Visiting Dr. *Williams*

VISITING **Dr. Williams**

Poems Inspired by the Life and Work of

William Carlos Williams

edited by Sheila Coghill & Thom Tammaro

foreword by Paul Mariani

UNIVERSITY OF IOWA PRESS · IOWA CITY

University of Iowa Press, Iowa City 52242

www.uiowapress.org
Printed in the United States of America
Design by Sara T. Sauers

The University of Iowa Press is a member of Green Press Initiative and is committed to preserving natural resources.

Printed on acid-free paper

Library of Congress Cataloging-in-Publication Data
Visiting Dr. Williams: poems inspired by the life and work of William Carlos Williams / edited by Sheila Coghill and Thom Tammaro; foreword by Paul Mariani.
p. cm.
Includes bibliographical references and index.
ISBN-13: 978-1-58729-986-5 (pbk.)
ISBN-10: 1-58729-986-0 (pbk.)
1. Williams, William Carlos, 1883–1963—Poetry. 2. American Poetry. 3. Poets—Poetry. I. Coghill, Sheila, 1952– II. Tammaro, Thom.
PS595.W44V57 2011
811'.608—dc22 2010048740

It is all
a celebration of the light.
—*William Carlos Williams*, "Asphodel, That Greeny Flower"

If it ain't a pleasure, it ain't a poem.
—*William Carlos Williams*

contents

PAUL MARIANI

The River of Language . . .

THE LANGUAGE, THE RIVER of language constantly washing over us, even in our sleep. In this, William Carlos Williams was no different from any young poet starting out who must try on any number of voices in order to discover those he or she could call one's own. He, too, ransacked the various anthologies of poets, settling on Keats among the English Romantics and Whitman among his American predecessors. And so he imitated them, turning out bad Keats and bad Whitman both: the doe-eyed lyric and the ersatz demotic. He learned what he could from his college friend Ezra Pound, two years his junior, who would soon shake the dust of America from his feet and sail for Venice and then London, to sit at the feet of Yeats, and insist that Bull Williams back there in Rutherford, New Jersey, do the same. In addition, he scolded Williams into reading Browning and the ballads and the prose of Henry James, as later he would champion Joyce and Eliot along with Wyndham Lewis and Ford Madox Ford. Here was the living vortex of language, to be found in Europe or among the work of Horace and Virgil or the author of "The Seafarer" or the medieval troubadours or Guido Cavalcanti or the Elizabethan lyricists who instinctively understood the meaning of melopoeia. And, farther afield, the ancient poetry of Japan and Cathay.

But those were still-living forces residing elsewhere and in other times, and—except for a year studying medicine in Leipzig and a visit to Rome to see his brother and another to London to meet up with Pound and a European sabbatical at forty—Williams remained here, in northern New Jersey and New York, interning at the old French Hospital and then Children's Hospital farther uptown, before setting up an office in his parents' house in Rutherford. But New York, too, in the years leading up to the Great War, like Chicago, was bristling with the arts and manifestoes and little magazines being printed in studios and sheds. There were the Manhattan salons, of course, and the art galleries, like the one run by the photographer Alfred Stieglitz and Georgia O'Keeffe. And there was the 1913 Armory Show, with its Cézannes and Matisses and Braques and Picassos, as well as the darker pigments of those New York tenement scenes and bars like McSorley's and ashcan back alleys, or those sweating boxers pummeling one another in the dense cigar smoke enveloping the spectral, leering onlookers.

And there was a new generation of American poets already searching—like Walt Whitman of Brooklyn before them—for what they took to be a distinctive American language: Robert Frost up in Massachusetts and New Hampshire, or Carl Sandburg and Vachel Lindsay out in Chicago, or the rhythm-and-blues-haunted Langston Hughes up in Harlem, or the Harvard poets like e. e. cummings and Wallace Stevens, or the bohemian voices of Maxwell Bodenheim and Alfred Kreymborg and Lola Ridge and Mina Loy, voices pulled under by the vast, impersonal currents of time.

Consider other revolutions of the time: the skyscraper and the new verticality as opposed to gewgaw Victoriana, the Ford flivver and the Detroit assembly lines that made that phenomenon possible, as well as canneries and assembly lines of every sort, from the East Coast to the West. Consider, too, the new journalism and the typographical revolutions and the portable typewriter with its return tab and lowercase words at the beginning of each line. Or—more massively—the Great War and the Russian Revolution, bringing with them a new darkness as well as new possibilities, including, for young Williams, a sense that the old forms—the blank verse line, the sonnet, the sestina, the villanelle, rhymed verse—ought to be replaced now with a sense of how the line might be formed and re-formed, broken or extended or drastically reduced. Had not Gertrude Stein blown apart traditional syntax in the same way that Braque and Picasso had blown apart the image, turning it into shards of intersecting color and design, or that Georges Antheil with his new music (replete with whirring propellers) had managed to shatter the sonic, in much the same way that our buzzing thoughts crossed and crisscrossed one another constantly, and without end? *Per omnia saecula saeculorum.*

And what of Joyce's *Ulysses*, which managed to catalog (and parody) every aspect of the English language from its Anglo-Saxon roots through Chaucer and Shakespeare and Milton and Pope and all the way through to the skritching riffs of New World jazz and the street slang of a living, breathing Anglo-Irish idiom in a way analogous to how St. Thomas Aquinas had with a jovial hullabaloo minutely examined the myriad layers of the language itself?

Break it, then, Williams came to understand—and practice—by the time he was thirty. Break the language and begin again and then begin again and again, in spite of Stevens warning him against doing just that, urging him to settle for a finished style instead. Cézanne, he might have said, rather than Juan Gris or Picasso. But what Williams wanted was to get back to the first forms of words and things, the language rinsed of its accumulated carbuncles of meaning, to see the thing itself, like Matisse intent on using a palette of primary colors only. Call it a river, then, the river of language, a living currency—yes, an imagined source of energy, but a living, vital currency of new coinage, too, and one of inestimable value: the language everywhere about him, with its complex rhythms, its sentences left unfinished because what had to be said had been said—and understood—before the sentence rounded on. . . . Words dancing with their one-two iambic patterns, or breaking against that, like a limping dog or an engorged satyr hobbling merrily along. Words counterpointed, contrapuntal, clashing against each other like atomic particles or drips and smatterings of far-flung paint, as in one of Jackson Pollack's action paintings, the white canvas becoming one mass of energy mimicking the imagination of the artist, the empty field becoming a mix of randomness and design dancing together. Paint itself. Words themselves. An energy force field released as light, charged uranium particles enlightening us, surprising us, the heady and erotic delight of the goddess revealed, and the poet helping us to see there the thing itself, the actual rose in the ceramic urinal (thank you, Marcel): the thing reimagined and reassembled, refreshed and rinsed and renewed, glazed now with a finish of rainwater, upon which, of course, so much depended.

Make it of this, then: of this and this and this, Williams insisted. Behold the world itself right there before one, here, now, in Paterson—the filthiest swill hole in all of America, as Williams himself once described it, but refreshed and fed by the waters of the Passaic, just as the Po fed Florence or the Seine Paris or the Thames London. True, the rivers had been degraded now by generations intent largely on buying and selling, just as the old myths of Greece and Rome had been degraded, though still—yes—capable of their original and elemental power and force and energy, like the Great Falls at Paterson with the currents running through and on farther down through Rutherford, where he'd been born and would practice medicine and deliver thousands of babies and eventually die eighty years on, while the river flowed on downstream through Newark—a city as inaptly named as New Haven—to merge forever with the flintbacked Atlantic.

It is this, then, that one comes to understand, the hunger for a living language to satisfy the imagination, a language shaped first by the particulars of time and history and place, and then—again—by the poet who listens that has appealed to so many American poets over the past hundred years. Hart Crane caught something of this in various sections of his epic *The Bridge*, as did the young Yvor Winters, early drawn to as later he would be repelled by what Williams insisted he had found. Stevens, too, who was of three minds about Wild Bill, that Carlos of the evanescent firefly candles, winking and twinkling. And H.D., too—who scolded Williams for spitting on the classic beauties he had wrought, only to abandon them in despair. And Marianne Moore, whom Williams saw as a brilliant sister in the search for a new way of saying. And of course his friend Ezra.

And then there were the younger poets, those who had schooled themselves first at the feet of Eliot and his American disciple Allen Tate, who then crossed over to Williams's side of the language divide sometime in the 1950s: Rexroth and Roethke, along with Lowell and Berryman and Randal Jarrell. And—within a few years—the river exponentially widening and deepening to include Allen Ginsberg and Charles Olson and Robert Creeley and Denise Levertov, as well as Paul Blackburn and Frank O'Hara and Amiri Baraka and Philip Levine and W. S. Merwin, along with Charles Tomlinson and David Ignatow and Cid Corman and Kenneth Koch and Joel Oppenheimer, and of course James Laughlin, Williams's publisher from the 1930s on.

And beyond these, other poets, too, who read Williams and found something there that resonated deeply with them, even when, as often happens, what they understood seems a misprision of the man. Still, something there struck deeply, as in the hollow of a bell, with Marvin Bell and Bill Heyen and Wendell Berry and Robert Bly and Charles Bernstein and Stephen Dunn and Clarence Major and Ed Hirsch.

The clipped, jagged line, the long line reminiscent of Whitman and Ford Madox Ford, the triadic step-down line, the variable foot, the subtle or jigging internal chiming keeping the ear deliciously off balance. And the living, breathing images of sycamores and locust trees; of meadow cattails and strewn petals along the falls; a man in an old army coat warming himself on a stoop in Paterson; a woman eating a plum or standing on one foot while peering into the cheap shoe for the tiny nail that has been bothering her; a girl walking down the street, quickly looking down at her own jiggling breasts hidden beneath her new sweater; a cat negotiating several pots on a shelf, one foot then the next; a fire engine racing down a New York City street, its sirens sounding and its bells clanging, then disappearing in the muffling gray of a cold, steady rain. Call it the Zen tactility of the thing itself. Call it one of Hopkins's inscapes observed and presented in words, minus only its anagogical component.

Say it, then: no ideas but in things. Some probe Dr. Williams for the way he managed to dissect and observe the living language, the language deconstructed then reconstructed: sounds puzzling and even mysterious in all their shimmering self-containment. Words like flickers of light emanating from the womblike alembic of the imagination separating out of the primordial chaos of the mind. And the poet's uncanny ability to present a century's-old scene—Paterson or Rutherford or New York, circa 1910 or 1920—as if no time had passed between then and now, as if the scene had been freshly painted with words only this morning. Still other poets wonder if anyone is really listening, if people ever take the time to actually see what is there before them, or can hear the music of the language about them, the thing itself lifted from the filthy river of desecrated time and rinsed clean and shining again as on the eighth day of creation. Persephone, Kora in hell, returning from the murkiness about us into the light again, if only for a moment, before she is pulled back under by the constant distractions of what passes for the quotidian, so that we die every day, again and again and again, for lack of the news, the real news, which only the poem can give us.

Make it of this, then, of this and this and this, poet, wherever you find yourself—in all senses of that phrase—like a lone star shining in the brilliant sunrise, toward which you add no part. So Williams, in his deep modesty and despair, believed, or seemed to believe, though something in him surely knew better. For he also understood that he was old rocky face, persisting even as the falls of the river rolled over his head like language itself—whether heard on the radio or television or read each day in the newspapers and the weeklies or—in our time—the blog-saturated word and the iPod, Facebook, and Skype, and whatever else is out there waiting to distract us. In spite of which he listened—and taught us to listen—for the dance of the syllables, the design of those authentic notes that somehow prevail against the insistent chatter that would drown us if it could.

William Carlos Williams

Refining the Pure Products of the American Grain

William Carlos Williams (1883–1963): he thought the most beautiful poem of the twentieth century was $E = MC^2$. His imagery flashes through the American psyche—imagistically, concretely, yet with significant and memorable impact. Grounded in the everyday world of objects, working-class people, and colloquial speech, Williams canonized modern America's fascination with materialism as embodying "no idea but in things." Things had life. Things had souls. Things were transcendent. William's influence on modern poetry and poets is ubiquitous yet subtle as light, transparent, a Vermeer interior. He also redefined the "thingness" of the American grain in a way writers came to see as transcendent, solid, albeit delivered in a red wheelbarrow full of apple blossoms, plums, Queen Anne's lace, wild carrot tops, and Breughel paintings. Williams delivered the news of modernism the same way, as a pediatrician, he delivered over 3,000 babies throughout his career. We hope *Visiting Dr. Williams: Poems Inspired by the Life and Work of William Carlos Williams* demonstrates the range of this influence.

Williams had a lifelong distaste for the expatriate modernism of T. S. Eliot and Ezra Pound, feeling they fetishized European culture, its literary standards, and its experimentations. Regardless of his own experimental poetic wanderings—from the epic five-volume *Paterson* to the epigrammatic "The Red Wheelbarrow" and "This Is Just to Say"—Williams always returned to the importance and beauty of concrete, visual objects that fired his imagination. Having met Williams when they were both undergraduates at the University of Pennsylvania, Pound, the arch-Svengali of modernism, recognized this quality early on and later paid homage to it in "Canto LXXVIII" (from *The Pisan Cantos*): ". . . as for the solidity of the white oxen in all this / perhaps only Dr. Williams . . . / will understand its importance, / its benediction." Likewise Katrina Vandenberg's "Plums" celebrates Williams's "This Is Just to Say": "Sweet plums of New Jersey the girls eat them at evening / they eat plums at midday and morning they eat plums at night / . . . Doctor Williams lives in the house with his poems he washes his hands / he washes his hands when it's too dark to write / he steps into the yard past the wheelbarrow bits of broken green bottle glass shining / he whistles the branches to rain down the plums / he whistles the branches to rain down the babies / he tells them the babies are plums." Immersed in the daily life of working-class people, Williams fine-tuned his ear for everyday speech, its rhythms, its surprising turns, its energy. Like Whitman, he advocated the use of colloquial speech, and he utilized it to release American poetry from the iambic prison that dominated and shrouded English verse since the Renaissance. To make the break with any and all influence, Williams, with Whitmanesque assertiveness, advises writers to "Quit hypnotizing yourself over the headlines; quit reading the papers. Pay attention to the bulletins of your art" (*Something to Say* 111).

These things, combined with his painterly rendering of modern urban settings, make his poetry attractive and accessible—not just an objet d'art. Working on separate continents, both Williams and Pound emphasized the need for radical innovation and a break from European literary traditions, particularly Romanticism. But like most modernists, Williams's idea of literary innovation was that it had to be a clear departure from the past. Modern poets should be creators (per Pound's dictum "Make it new"). Imitating a dead poet was, in their thinking, imitating a dead tradition—and soon one's own writing would become dead and deadening as well. Having resolved this issue of "the anxiety of influence," contemporary poets honor Williams's use of capturing scenes of life, of familiar, ordinary things, as if suspended in time (like stop-frame photography). And for Williams, this meant utilizing his much-beloved trees and flowers, the world of nature. In "Saxifrage: To the Memory of William Carlos Williams," Susan Glickman observes, "Only the imagination is real! You declared it / time and again. But truth / is always stranger. . . . Saxifrage my flower, that splits the rock." In the same vein, Eleanor Berry observes in "Taking the Field," "They have all gone over to wild carrot—all / the fields left untilled, . . . all the flowers have gone / to seed, the creamy *Queen Anne's lace* / have become brown *birds' nests*." And Kay Boyle echoes Williams's love of nature as a canvas of the imagination in "Two Twilights for William Carlos Williams": "Here where I live / The birds speak in a shower of voices / . . . The evening stillness fluid with / These liquid tongues / That run like silver water to / The island of the heart."

Williams knew from firsthand experience that the harshness of everyday life could not—nor should be—overlooked or romanticized away: suspicion or disdain directed at new immigrants trying to better themselves; domestic tragedy in the form of stillbirth; family tensions; couples locked in mute restlessness and dissatisfaction; covetousness; and serial infidelity. After completing his medical studies, Williams married Florence Herman (Flossie) in 1912. They had two sons, William Eric (1914) and Paul (1916). They lived, worked, and raised their family in the house at 9 Ridge Road in Rutherford, New Jersey—the same house in which Williams practiced medicine throughout his career and to which dozens of poets made their pilgrimage during his lifetime. In the course of his practice, he witnessed the darker side of familiar and everyday life. In Heid E. Erdrich's "Some Elsie," we see acknowledgment of Williams's struggle with America's less attractive side: "And there she sits, Elsie, in American Lit., / at the Community College or Harvard or the U. / The sleek New York TA reads how her family / 'married with a dash of Indian Blood' / and thus escaped the fate of the 'pure products' / Wm. Carlos Wms. saw go crazy." Likewise, in "WCW" Maxine Kumin observes: "and remember him for / his revulsion against fascism / his admiration for the workingclass / women whose babies he brought forth / often after hours of harsh labor / and most of all hold fast / the freshness of the unadorned / and potent plain American / speech that he saluted in his poems."

Loved for his decidedly American voice, for his insightful rendering of both the light and dark in American society, and for his advocacy of young, emerging writers, Williams left an indelible mark on modern poetry that continues into the twenty-first century. But as attractive and accessible as readers think of Williams's better-known poems, unlike his contemporaries, he was not sufficiently (in his mind) "recognized" as an accomplished poet in his time. He did receive notable awards, among them the Bollingen Prize for Literature (1952). But until he died, Williams felt underappreciated. He was conflicted about this. This, too, a thread in the fabric of the American psyche—its Puritan suspicion of artists and works of the imagination, yet its wholehearted support for any activity that was "useful" and made money. Yet among his poet-colleagues, Williams's significance was felt and understood. Less than a year after his death, the *Beloit Poetry Journal* (14, no. 1 [Fall 1963]) published a special issue, "William Carlos Williams: A Memorial Chapbook," edited by David Ignatow, though, as Ignatow writes, the chapbook "was conceived during Williams' last year with no thought of his approaching death." Ignatow continues: "Many of us were aware of the seriousness of his illness which had deprived him of the use of his right arm. His speech had been severely impaired. He was in a depressed mood and had virtually given up any attempt to continue writing, but so strong was the influence of Williams, the doer, that we received the news of our eyes and ears through the pulsation of his lines. We saw and heard him fighting, buoyant, unshaken and undefeated. It was the occasion for a chapbook of poems in joyful hailing of the man and his life." And we are delighted to include here some of the poems that appeared in that memorial chapbook.

Williams saw the irony in this, the double-edged sword embodied in money (which gave one leisure to pursue art). In wry commentary, Edward Hirsch articulates this in "Liberty Brass": "I was sitting across from the rotating sign / . . . *Automatic Screw Machine Products* / And brooding about our fathers / Always on the make to make more money." Adding to the irony—especially of an artist forgotten as well as whose memory is obliterated in his own hometown—Paul Mariani expresses this melancholy everyday fact in "Elegy for William Carlos Williams on the Eve of His 125th Birthday": "A chic Italian restaurant here on Rutherford's / Park Avenue. On the corner across the street: / your home, sold to strangers. All those bright / flowers you & Flossie tended to in your back yard / gone. . . . listening as you taught me with the one good ear / I've left for the river's sad and distant music riffing / those jagged Jersey sounds you loved so well."

And finally the sad irony is that many artists are *not* recognized until after their death. Allen Ginsberg's "Death News" begins shaping and memorializing Williams's presence in American poetry: ". . . He isn't dead / as the many pages of words arranged thrill / with his intonations the mouths of meek kids / becoming subtle even in Bengal." Expanding on this idea, Marvin Bell enlarges Williams's contribution to redefining the American grain in "The Book of the Dead Man (The Red Wheelbarrow)": "The dead man hears them talking of 'The Red Wheelbarrow.' / He hears Williams say, 'The word is not the thing.' / To the dead man, the poem is itself, a dance, a complex of the sensory at a distance neither of time nor of space."

By the end of his life, it was clear that Williams was truly a poet of the twentieth century whose life and work would continue to influence the trajectory of American poetry as it arced toward the millennium. And now, more than a decade into the twenty-first century, it is clear that Williams is a poet of the twenty-first century as well, his influence yet to be fully realized, as each successive generation of poets discovers the "new" that lives within his work. Although the earliest poem collected here is Ernest Walsh's sonnet "Doctor Bill Williams," written in the 1920s, the most recent are Joseph Massey's Williams-inspired and contoured sequence "From a Window" and Joe Milutis's "By Defective Means," from *New Jersey as an Impossible Object*, "an ongoing multimedia project that uses Williams's *Paterson* as a psychogeographical map for the city Paterson and documents the resonant space between the poem and its restless referent with audio, video, photos, and commentary that will culminate in a large-scale audio piece," both of which pull Williams into the wired twenty-first century—evidence of Williams's durability, expansiveness, and continuing presence.

The poems collected here represent but a small percentage of poems that have been inspired by the life and work of William Carlos Williams. Given Williams's continuing presence in contemporary poetry, we can only imagine the poems yet to be written, the conversations yet to be had. In a more perfect world, space limitations, economics, and estate litigation would not exist, allowing us to include all the poems that we hoped to include. Nevertheless, we hope that *Visiting Dr. Williams* reflects not only Williams's centrality to American poetry—past and present—but also to its future.

As with all projects like this one, there are many people to thank. We would like to begin by thanking the writers who have shown us generosity, support, enthusiasm, and patience during the editing process. We would also like to thank the editors and publishers who helped arrange permission to reprint many of these poems. Also, we are indebted to the individuals who have assisted us—each in his or her own special way. For their special interest in the anthology and their assistance, a special thanks to: Bob Arnold, Longhouse Publishers and Booksellers; Michael Basinski, curator, The Poetry Collection at the University of Buffalo; Carlos T. Blackburn; Ianthe Brautigan; Stephen Burt; Bryce Conrad, editor, and Todd Giles, associate editor, *WCW Review*; Ian Copestake, president, WCW Society; Fredrick T. Courtright, The Permissions Company and permissions dude extraordinaire; Sidney Dreese, archivist, Gingrich Library, Albright College; Peggy Fox, president, and Quinn Marshall, permissions editor, New Directions Publishing Corp.; Peter Gizzi; Yaedi Ignatow; Theresa Maier; Paul Merchant, director, and Kim Stafford of the William Stafford Archives; Thomas

Meyer; Barry Moser and Cara Moser at Pennyroyal Press; Alice Notely; Laura Ruby; Susan Solt; Robert Stanton; and Jill Turnbull.

We are especially honored and grateful to Paul Mariani for his support and for taking time from his busy schedule of writing, editing, and teaching to write the foreword and for offering his poem. As always, we are grateful to Holly Carver, former director of the University of Iowa Press, and to her small but enormously talented staff for their enthusiasm, professionalism, attention, and support throughout this project.

At Minnesota State University Moorhead, we are most grateful to Shelly Heng and her staff of work-study students for assisting us in preparing the manuscript and for all-around organization; at Livingston Lord Library: Stacey Voeller, electronic resources librarian; Dianne Schmidt, library technician in the Interlibrary Loan Department; and Kathy Ness, library technician, for their good spirits and patience with us and for their help in tracking down numerous poems and rare and out-of-print books in a timely manner. Thanks, too, to Brooke Kramer and Julie Larson Walnum for their careful proofreading of the manuscript.

We are also grateful to our many students, especially those in Thom's fall 2006 senior capstone seminar, "In the American Grain: Frost, Williams, and the American Modernist Moment," for teaching us about Williams and his work. It certainly was a pleasure.

Visiting Dr. *Williams*

WCW

I turned in
by the bayshore
and parked,
the crosswind
hitting me hard
side the head,
the bay scrappy
and working:
what a
way to read
Williams! till
a woman came
and turned
her red dog loose
to sniff
(and piss
on)
the dead horseshoe
crabs.

The Carlos Poems

They become kindred spirits
in a land overflowing with ghosts. Kindred spirits in a dying
sun's world.—Adrian C. Louis

The first visit

Hello, William Carlos Williams, you've come
calling, at last! Last night, that dream about

you woke me up! We were somewhere—you said,
"fuck it, break speed limits, blur the landscape."

I remember looking into your mouth. Your
ghostly teeth were glowing like the back of

eucalyptus leaves in a thunderstorm.
But William, how was I supposed to know

that your middle name Carlos meant *Carlos*,
like the name of some cousins? You, the *most*

American of poets according
to critics! You, *amigo*, who upon

seeing the Caribbean for the first
time "wanted to cradle it like a blue

seashell, like any other dumb tourist. . . ."
You were half-Puertorriqueño? Let's take

a walk. Let's walk past the open windows
of undergraduates with shut eyelids.

These poor students have tired themselves out
listening to *Belly*, *Morrissey*, *Butthole*

Surfers, *Throwing Muses*, *Dead Kennedys*.
There's a Chicano rapper now, *Kid Frost*:

no more silence for *la raza* (*Carlos*,
that's the people), for any one of us.

You are one of us if only by blood.
Look, William, you still have a shadow, your

many words on many pages. I love
what you asked me in the dream this morning:

"If you must own an aquarium why not
fill it up with expensive champagne?"

Ah, *amigo*! Already the daylight
chases you away: not yet, *por favor*!

Unhatted as we are, we dare not
walk any further towards what is

on the next block, and the next, and the next.
You smile at me. I make you remember

something: hunger, youth, time, the need to need.
Adios, goodbye, yes this is right, William

Carlos Williams, *a-dios*, go back to your God.

The second visit

You follow me to a matinee, sit
in the row behind me; funny, *Dead Again*.

Carlito, that's Andy Garcia. I
don't know why he is with rich, white people

without them noticing his lovely brown
skin, his blue-black hair, head shaped like a bell.

He is not trying to pass as white; were you?
You did pass as an American, as the

North American. You did publish as an
American, judged the *Pisan Cantos*

as what an American citizen speaks.
Andy Garcia is fistfighting with

British Kenneth Branaugh over the soul
—and the body that comes with it—of a

beautiful woman. Was Pygmalion
the inspiration for the Statue

of Liberty? William, alive again,
but so are young lovers here in this dark

theater with us, feeling each other up
as if dreaming with eyes and legs open.

A lover (such a lovely word, *lover*)
said to me: "Is that a revolution

in your pants or are you just happy to
see me?" See how silliness is such an

American patent? Let's go. No, no,
Carlos, this isn't porno. Do you

know the term *blue movie*? Delicious, no?
English, what a magician you are

on good days. Blue movies make me think of blue
bodies: the waving of blue feet, dancing

blue arms, the rubbing of blue chests and breasts,
the kissing of blue hands. It's not like that;

it's never like that. Let us meditate
on popcorn, the seats, shoes, rows, aisles, curtains,

the American flag in the corner,
ushers, spilled Good & Plentys, screen scratches,

exit signs. Andy Garcia is fading.
The movie is over; then, the sudden

ordinary light of the world, our world,
burns with meaning and power. Look at me

talking to a ghost instead of working.
But perhaps this is my work. What is

poetry if it isn't the public
memory of a night wasted singing?

Carlos, to quote Doris Day, *que será,*
será. *Ser* is the verb *to be*. You were.

I hope to be. How to part from you? Ah,
mi casa es su casa which roughly

translates as *my poem is your poem*.

The Thief of Poetry

To you
my friend who
was in this

street once
were on it
getting

in with it
getting on with
though

only passing by
a smell of hamburgers
that day

an old mattress
and a box spring
as it

darkened
filling the empty
rumble

of a street
in decay of time
it fell out that

there was no
remaining
whether out of a wish

to be moving on
or frustrated
willingness to stay

here to stand
still
the moment

had other plans
and now in this
jungle of darkness

the future still makes plans
O ready to go
Conceive of your plight

more integrally
the snow
that day

buried all but the most obtuse
only the most generalized
survives

the low profile
becomes a constant again
the line of ocean

of shore
nestling
confident

impermanent
to rise again
in new

vicissitude
in explicit
triumph

drowns the hum
of space
the false point

of the stars
in specific
new way of happening

Now
no one remembers
the day you walked a certain distance

along the beach
and then
walked back

it seems
in your tracks
because it

was ending
for the first time
yes but now

is another way of
spreading out
toward the end

the linear style
is discarded
though this is

not realized for centuries
meanwhile
another way of living had come and gone

leaving its width
behind
now the tall cedars

had become locked into
the plan
so that everywhere

you looked
was burning
inferential

interior space
not for colonies
but already closed

turned in on itself
its back
as beautiful as the sea

where you go up
and say the word
eminence

to yourself
all was lived in
had been lived in

was coming to an end
again
in the featureless present

that was expanding to
cloister it
this just a little too

comic parable
and so insure the second
beginning

of that day seen against the street
of whichever way
you walked and talked

knowing not knowing
the thing that was describing you
and not knowing

your taller
well somehow more informed
bearing

as you wind down
only a second
it did matter

you come back so seldom
but it's all right
the way of staying

you started comes back
procession into the fire
into the sky

the dream you lost
firm in its day
reassured and remembered

Appetite

Of course you ate the plums
she was saving for breakfast,
you were always selfish that way,
and on the weekends
you happily cranked up your Model T Ford
and drove away from the practice, the patients,
the neighbors, your wife,
your wheels crushing the fallen leaves.
You drove right out of your life,
across the bridge and into the city
where everything exciting was,
the women, speakeasies, the jazz clubs,
and you ate it all up
because you knew when you crossed the bridge
again into the familiar streets,
still reeking of sweet wine and smoke,
she would be waiting to take your overcoat
and hat, waiting with the children
in the laundry or in the garden,
she would be waiting to forgive you,
because that's what she did,
and you, you ate it all up.

William Carlos Williams Back in Puerto Rico

Well Jersey is still a yellow place
May comes to with rain washing

chickens and pots of flowers
and New England–delicate rust

and immaculate white beds—
but back in old San Jaun

it's beautiful as a baseball
game or Spanish Jews—I have some

of their blood too—escaping
laughing from the Inquisition.

Here slums are magnificent
baroque and golden red stone,

and what makes me happier than
the Pleiades is the skinny rubber tree

with big boobs and milk under
the skin all out in my back

yard or up in the tropical rain
forest. There pines are friends

and cool even to cranky old men
named Alfredo or Carlos

who walk with shaggy nostalgia
like the poor ascending home

where they listen to the radio,
make love, and iron new clothes.

Prescriptions

When the pen pushes down on the pad,
indentations form the hieroglyph believed
by generations to be the finished product
of a brilliant mind. What they don't see
are the half-uttered words clipped short,
scratched out and begun again, over and
over. What they don't smell is the oil
leaking from the car that has stopped at
that stop light just long enough to note
that "so much depends." So much depends
upon a moment, a chance encounter, a
phrase or the way Flossie's plums would
have tasted if only he had arrived in time
to take one from the bowl to his lips,
those same lips that utter the words scrawled
across a pad in the morning, typed and
retyped in the evening. Notice
the trace of a hand that existed once.
Follow where it leads.

What I Know about Poetry

for William Carlos Williams & Jonathan Williams

Bindweed grabs
the cornstalk not
to strangle
but
to blossom.
Honeysuckle trips
the walker
so he
falls.

Thus:
to smell the sweet

flowers
near
the intelligent
lowly
ground.

The Book of the Dead Man (The Red Wheelbarrow)

Live as if you were already dead.
—Zen admonition

1. About the Dead Man and "The Red Wheelbarrow"

The dead man has been asked about a red wheelbarrow.
Not an actual wheelbarrow, not the thing itself.
The dead man has been asked about the thought of the barrow.
Not of a pushcart, not of the gardener, not of the farmer.
This red wheelbarrow sits pristine after rain.
The dead man can tell it is spring and all, it's the rain.
The dead man, stopping at the Williams home, read the medical shingle.
He did not take down the shingle and carry it to the classroom.
He did not bring the wheelbarrow to school.
Later, the dead man took *Spring & All* to Spain, the one book only.
He had time there to let the little wheelbarrow sit unused.
Thus did the dead man restore the dance of the red wheelbarrow.
Thus did he peel the layers of claptrap.
The dead man flexes his muscles, peels his eyes, licks his lips, sniffs
briefly and opens his ears.
Then he takes the handles of the red wheelbarrow.

2. More About the Dead Man and "The Red Wheelbarrow"

The dead man hears them talking of "The Red Wheelbarrow."
He hears Williams say, "The word is not the thing."
To the dead man, the poem is itself, a dance, a complex of the sensory
at a distance neither of time nor of space.
Albeit, it is as well a piece in a jigsaw of the imagination and a credo born
of desire.

The dead man hath interred in the classroom the canon.
The dead man does not cease his dancing to name the tune.
The dead man places the red wheelbarrow next to a red wagon, in the
garage with the silver roller skates, near a scooter made from a
vegetable crate.
It is so clean, this unreal wheelbarrow, wetted, waiting, sacramental.
The dead man can hold in mind a red wheelbarrow and a blue guitar at
the same time.
They are equally light in the ether.
Stevens was music, Williams was dance, the wheelbarrow was red.
The dead man rode the wheelbarrow and picked the guitar.
The dead man heard the music of the spheres even as he felt, also, the
dance of the galaxies.
The dead man need not defend his turf, for he has drawn no boundary.
So much depended on the poem having no title.

For Bill Charley Bill on Memorial Day

Steven Willett asks for "objective standards for assessing the poet's handling of rhythmic [structures]" after remarking: "aside from its lack of memorability, which no one seems inclined to dispute, only to deprecate, free verse. . . ."

I dispute
that &

celebrate it.
What I

am suggesting
is that

some nonmetrical
& polymetrical

poetry makes
memorable, even

indelible, a
range of

acoustic and
linguistic &

semantic experiences
that is

equal, for
its engaged

listeners and
readers, to

any other
type of

poetry. But
at the

same time
I categorically

dispute an
intrinsic value

to a
poem's memorizability,

as I
would find

it absurd
to profess

intrinsic value
for the

opposite. Moreover,
I would

question the
idea of

intrinsic values
of this

type at
all, just

as I
would reject

the idea
that poetic

value has
some intimate

connection with
objective standards

of assessment,
which are

likely more
useful for

business accounting
than for

aesthetic projects.
There's no

formula for
poetry: constraints

or not
countable rhythms

or uncountable
(and unaccountable)

ones. Yet
there's a

memorable sadness
to this

refusal of
the contemporary,

or the
idea that

it was
(or is)

so much
better then

or over
there (over

there) as
if right

now words
don't form

and reform
in patterns

that mock
those can

or will
no longer

perform them.

Sonnet XV

In Joe Brainard's collage its white arrow
He is not in it, the hungry dead doctor.
Of Marilyn Monroe, her white teeth white—
I am truly horribly upset because Marilyn
and ate King Korn popcorn," he wrote in his
of glass in Joe Brainard's collage
Doctor, but they say "I LOVE YOU"
and the sonnet is not dead.
takes the eyes away from the gray words,
Diary. The black heart beside the fifteen pieces
Monroe died, so I went to a matinee B-movie
washed by Joe's throbbing hands. "Today
What is in it is sixteen ripped pictures
does not point to William Carlos Williams.

Taking the Field

a field
of the wild carrot taking
the field by force
—William Carlos Williams

They have all gone over to wild carrot—all
the fields left untilled, ungrazed, the lots
still vacant in the new industrial subdivisions,
the unmowed roadsides. And now, at this
far end of summer, all the flowers have gone
to seed, the creamy *Queen Anne's lace*
have become brown *birds' nests*, lined
each with dozens of small, bristle-covered seeds
that catch on your sleeve as you pass,
ride home with you.

New, each umbel lay open
to the sky, a circle of white pages around
a central spot of purple. Now they curl
in upon themselves, but still
keep casting off their bristly seeds,
poems importuning audience, insistent
on lodging in minds that will carry them
to far roadsides, sow them in distant fields.

In a Motel Parking Lot, Thinking of Dr. Williams

I.

The poem is important, but
not more than the people
whose survival it serves,

one of the necessities, so they may
speak what is true, and have
the patience for beauty: the weighted

grainfield, the shady street,
the well-laid stone and the changing tree
whose branches spread above.

For want of songs and stories
they have dug away the soil,
paved over what is left,

set up their perfunctory walls
in tribute to no god,
for the love of no man or woman,

so that the good that was here
cannot be called back
except by long waiting, by great

sorrows remembered and to come
by invoking the thunderstones
of the world, and the vivid air.

II.

The poem is important,
as the want of it
proves. It is the stewardship

of its own possibility,
the past remembering itself
in the presence of

the present, the power learned
and handed down to see
what is present

and what is not: the pavement
laid down and walked over
regardlessly—exiles, here

only because they are passing.
Oh remember the oaks that were
here, the leaves, purple and brown,

falling, the nuthatches walking
headfirst down the trunks,
crying "onc! onc!" in the brightness

as they are doing now
in the cemetery across the street
where the past and the dead

keep each other. To remember,
to hear and remember, is to stop
and walk on again

to a livelier, surer measure.
It is dangerous
to remember the past only

for its own sake, dangerous
to deliver a message
you did not get.

Dream Song #324: An Elegy for W.C.W., the lovely man

Henry in Ireland to Bill underground:
Rest well, who worked so hard, who made a good sound
constantly, for so many years:
your high-jinks delighted the continents & our ears:
you had so many girls your life was a triumph
and you loved your one wife.

At dawn you rose & wrote—the books poured forth—
you delivered infinite babies, in one great birth—
and your generosity
to juniors made you deeply loved, deeply:
if envy was a Henry trademark, he would envy you,
especially the being through.

Too many journeys lie for him ahead,
too many galleys & page-proofs to be read,
he would like to lie down
in your sweet silence, to whom was not denied
the mysterious late excellence which is the crown
of our trials & our last bride.

Phone Call to Rutherford

"It would be—
                    a mercy if
you did not come
                    see me . . .

"I have dif-fi / cul-ty
                    s/peaking, I
cannot count on it, I
am afraid it would be too em-
barrassing f f—
                    for me ."

                    —Bill, can you still
                    answer letters?

"No . my hands
are tongue-tied
You have . . . made

a record in my heart .
                    Goodbye ."

A Dream of William Carlos Williams

You were dead, but how sleek and darkly calm you were!
"There is some change," I said. Your wife said,
"There is a big change!" A third person was with us—
We all laughed about form, how sweet it is, *what*
It is! While you laughed, your rocker broke. "You fell

Out of it!" I shouted, but you were startled
To think of leaving form. As we walked out
The back door and down the wooden stoop,
You asked about form in my poems. I found myself
Lying, saying I cared nothing about form. . . .

Two Twilights for William Carlos Williams

Here where I live
The birds speak in a shower of voices
In the trees at dusk, taking
Sweet-tongued decisions about north or south,
Or near or far,
The evening stillness fluid with
These liquid tongues
That run like silver water to
The island of the heart.

Both twilights bring this multitudinous whispering
Across the cove,
A music spuming from the quiet leaves
At dawn, at dusk. Here in the open window
The stars fade as the first birds' voices call,
The birds' tongues cease at the coming of the stars.

September 3 (The Dr. William Carlos Williams Mistake)

I had severe insomnia last night with
the past, the present and the future detailing
themselves
like: Oh, the shit we run through our minds!
Then I remembered that it was Dr. William Carlos
Williams' birthday and that made me feel better
until almost dawn.

Note:

September 3 is not
Dr. William Carlos Williams'
birthday. It is the birthday
of a girlfriend.
Dr. William Carlos Williams
was born on September 17, 1883.

Interesting mistake.

The Influence of William Carlos Williams

He cannot help this time. I am to blame,
Dreaming of the dead physician-poet,
Immortal lines within a story frame
Inside the office of his old estate

On 9 Ridge Road in Rutherford. I'm eight:
He's swabbing me with cotton, arm aflame;
I watch him push the needle in, and wait:
He cannot help this time. I am to blame,

Drawing on his influence, mere phantasm,
As he draws blood from me, inoculates
Against the influenzas of acclaim.
Dreaming of the dead physician-poet,

I open envelopes and veins of fate
On the gurney. He listens to the iambs
Of my ordinary heart to demonstrate
Immortal lines within a story frame:

He aims a penlight at the inner drum
Of my ear and shakes his head, irrigates
My tongue and then depresses it: inflamed.
Inside the office of his old estate,

My poems lie in piles. The doctor states
Prognoses candidly and puts the blame
On too much Milton, far too little Yeats,
On too much meter, an overdose of rhyme:
He cannot help this time.

Bicentennial

This official bicentennial arts person programming
state-wide culturals for the up and coming
year-long Fourth of July, made an appointment,
and came, and I said I would (what I could),
and she said, "Are there any other New Jersey
poets we should mention?" and I said,
"Well, William Carlos Williams to start." And she:
"Has he published books?"
And I saw hall on hall
of stone glass buildings, a million offices
with labels on glass doors. And at the first desk
in every office, nothing. And beyond, in the inner
office, nothing. And a lost wind going, and doors
all swinging bang in the wind and swinging bang.
And at the end of every corridor
a wall of buttons blinking data dead.

"WCW & Mary O"

We stood up to go—

Bill too—wavering
and fragile—once straight

and tall—but when I

kissed him it was—as
it always had been—

is—a young man's kiss.

For W.C.W.

The rhyme is after
all the repeated
insistence.

There, you say, and
there, and there,
and *and* becomes

just so. And
what one wants is
what one wants,

yet completely
as you
say.

Let's
let it go.
I want—

Then there is—
and,
I want.

Alicia Silverstone Meets William Carlos Williams

This is, like
just to say?
You know
those plums?
in the
refrigerator?
that you were
saving?
for breakfast?
Whatever.
They were like
so delicious?
so sweet?
and, you know,
so cold?

Confession

Forgive me
they were delicious
—William Carlos Williams

Like Williams and his plums, meat
turning to sugar under skin, I confess

my sin: I've eaten the apples
that ferment in tall grass, abandoned

when the life fell out of the place.
With the first cold days, at night

they freeze, then thaw a bit by noon,
last warmth of October

drawing these few incorrigible bees
who still bother to venture across

this rotting round globe.

Williams Was Wrong

Now I find peace in everything around me;
in the modest campion and the shoals of light
leaping across the swaying sea
and the gulls gliding out of sight.
The tops of wave-confettied rocks
slide into water and turn into seals.
They move to the lively reel
of the cove's clapping dance hall,
rising blithe yelps above the sea's music.
The ocean draws in and out like an accordion
and unseen lithe fingers play the strings
of joy on what the moment brings.
The seals close and part and close again.
Their awkward fins have turned to wings.

In Defense of Forest Lawn

In his poem "Tract" William Carlos Williams
recommends a style for funerals
much like the style he practiced
as a poet: a "rough plain hearse"
resembling a farm wagon, its driver
demoted to walk alongside holding the reins,
and the mourners riding after
with conspicuous inconvenience, open
"to the weather as to grief."

In horse-and-buggy days, perhaps,
such a scenario might have worked,
but nowadays much-weathered wood denotes
deluxe accommodations. A triumph
for Williams' esthetics, but the problem
remains: how to bury people simply
and tastefully, without on the one hand
holding up traffic unduly or on the other
treating the corpse like industrial waste.

Personally I think Forest Lawn
has got just about the right combination
of hokum and expedience, gravitas and pizazz.
People are inclined to laugh at Forest Lawn,
having been instructed by Evelyn Waugh
that only the sovereign Pontiff can *own*
the Pietà, that Europe has the copyright
on class, and that Americans had better stick
to. . . What would he suggest: farm wagons?

But if Romans did well to copy Greek originals,
if museums needn't be embarrassed by their casts—
if, that is, form and not seignoralty
is our ideal, then why shouldn't Forest Lawn
heap as much of the enmarbled past
on the plates of our grief as, say
Westminster Abbey or St. Paul's? Why shouldn't
the dead, God damn it, be allowed one Parthian
shot at greatness? Aren't wakes for feasting?

Suppose we did it in the minimalist way
Williams suggests, bankrupting florists
and stonecutters. Do you think the heirs
in their enhanced prosperity would endow
posterity with anything so grand or lush
as a properly got-up cemetery? Think again.
How, I wonder, did Waugh himself get planted?
Opulently, I'm sure. So, gentlemen, if you'll step
Over here, I'd like to show you our brochure.

A Physical Moon beyond Paterson

William Carlos Williams had finished
His mid-December rounds
In an old hospital made of fieldstones.
He walked out into the late-afternoon sun
And sat in his car, an emerald Hudson.
He said *no* twice and straightened,
The car slowly going down the rural hill.
He saw a row of technicians dressed in lead coats
And yesterday's baby with a bowel obstruction.
All of the previous night
This road was plowed. The snow
Climbing six feet now on either side.
With little warning a hot spike
Had entered his elbow. He had suffered a stroke.
Maybe he was lost for oxygen; some odd gaiety
Overwhelmed him while descending a winter hill.
He began to play the green Hudson
Violently against the two walls of snow,
Leaving the seasonal paint of the car
On a quarter mile of water turned crystal.
Accelerating, he shot across the state highway
Coming to rest in a marsh with a deep brook.
He was crying and singing, awake
With the spongy earth below him.
He was not the Polish woman of his night-calls:
She endured two hours of labor
Scouring her kitchen floor. She curtsied
And froze, delivering in that position
A seven-pound girl.

And that's the glory. For a moment
This old man was a rough sluice of toboggan
Gone tobogganing.
And then he just walked out across
The colossal toxic wilderness of New Jersey.
The holiest dish to whiteness passing over . . .

Memory

A kind of achievement, William Carlos Williams said. Or a curse, said the man who couldn't get the phone book out of his head. Speak, Nabokov asked of his. Which it tends to, if we invoke it often enough. Imagination is its most important friend, selecting, coloring, casting aside. Without imagination, an endlessness, like my colleague's story of his summer by the lake when he listed birds and his wife was tortured by a lingering cold; he told me so much I didn't know what I'd been told. More and more I forget what I need, and remember what I'd like to forget. And sometimes I keep talking, keep recalling, as a way of not saying what I feel. Memory's law: what we choose to say about our past becomes our past. That other past, the one we've lived, exists in pieces that flicker and grow dim. I can buy memory in a store called Circuit City. I can press search, and find a fact, a person, but not what I've most dearly lost. Every time I save I exclude.

To William Carlos Williams

I would make this all as single as a song,
My own assumption in a flittering stance,
Twenty years cast in an easy affirmation.

The truth is there is truth on every side,
Each protagonist as relativist
Invests the present with his intellectual twist.

You are no absolute, Bill! But genial soul
And spanking eye, no hatred of your fellows,
Concludes we love you the worldly American.

With gusto to toss the classics out, and with them
The sonnet, you live yet in a classic Now,
Pretend to advance order in your plain music,

And even preach that Form (you call it measure,
Or idiom) is all, albeit your form would mate
The sprawling forms, inchoate, of our civilization.

Some Elsie

And there she sits, Elsie, in American Lit.,
at the Community College or Harvard or the U.
The sleek New York TA reads how her family
"married with a dash of Indian Blood"
and thus escaped the fate of the "pure products"
Wm. Carlos Wms. saw go crazy.

Does she sit, terrified or transfixed?
Waiting for someone to turn, look at her and think,
There she is, that Elsie.
So what if she was hemmed all around with murder?
Or if a few of her relatives had screws loose?
She'd deny bathing in filth from Friday to Sunday.
What a girl does on the weekend,
come on now, that's her own affair.

She endures the comments about her body,
"the great ungainly hips and flopping breasts."
What if her ample chest had been her pride?
What if, at first, she flushed at the sound of
"voluptuous water" and took it as a compliment?

What if, at first she thought, *Ah, at last*
a poem about someone I know.
Imagining that she'd strain after deer, too,
if stuck in the suburbs passing pills.
But now, even knowing her hips,
somehow become, the TA says, *a text,*
doesn't help the sting when she thinks
there's some truth she'd like to express,
broken brain or not.

Call Me Pier

I have just returned from a visit to my pier
For a long time I would go to pier early
So much depends upon a pier
This is an old pier
I celebrate my pier, and what I assume . . .
I had a pier
There is a certain slant of pier
On woman's first disobedience, and the pier
Christmas won't be Christmas without the pier
I wandered lonely as a pier
Pier was spiteful
This is just to say I have eaten the pier

Slow Rain, October

Minds like beds are always made up
—William Carlos Williams

Oh to dive into an unmade bed and sleep,
and sleep, and sleep. The room is shadowy,
covers piled in a heap with pillows
still scrunched up, one halfway down the mattress
for my knees, two near the wall for our heads.
Outside, leaves draw closer, and as night
seeps from the forest, spills over the wet

back yard, climbs the stairs to the deck,
spreads its cloak and foggy stars across the window,
I die now for a little while: even the family photos
in the Welsh cabinet by the bed are strange to me—
parents marrying, parents aging, children small,
children grown, husband and wife
(that's I) embracing—sixty years of family.

Sweetness of not making the bed today,
not making the body today, not making
the life today. The pilot light flickers in the heater,
source of warmth in the old beaded-board house
with its drafts and cracks and currents.
Three white roses on the Welsh cabinet
open further, ripen, slacken, begin to bruise.

Ars Poetica on Lava

So much depends . . .
—William Carlos Williams

The night I picked my way
across the lava slicked by rain
in the moonless dark, all past
and future sliced away
like bread. Nothing existed
but the blade of my held breath
and the flashlight probing
the black and roiling rock
for a safe place to place
a sneaker down. One shoe
after the other, disembodied
from the feet they were tied to,
with orders to swing out, land,
grip, and pass me on.

Two hours it took to cross
that stretch of Stygian black,
having no thought but the need
to prevail, upright. Now I know
what it means to balance
a writer's life. Each footfall,
each stopping point, a fulcrum
around which the body teeters
and sways: a high-wire act
demanding concentration—
the chattering mind delivered up
blank as cardboard with a pinhole,
dependent, in the pit-dark, upon one
thin thread of dazzle coming through.

Williams in Autumn

all to no end save beauty
—AT THE BALLGAME

October 4, 1961:
The hawkweed is bristling
In the Jersey meadows
And the sidewalks of East Rutherford
Are littered, here
And there, with hulls
From the horse chestnut trees.

The end of summer
Is no poorer for any of that.
The cemetery's snow-faced doughboy
Stands overlooking the pastures
Of his republic,
And at 9 Ridge Road
The old poet,

Beautiful and bare of poetry,
Has finally declined to rummage
Through the welter of his years.
He is tired of being a house
Whose rooms are closing,
Stroke by stroke,
And wants now simply to sit

Bathing in the light
He thinks is falling for him
For the last time on Yankee Stadium,
Flooding the shapes of the players,

And spilling into his room.
A game he wrote was *close*
to the principles of physics

and lyric poetry.
Four innings later
New York breaks on top,
One to nothing, Ford's unfurling body
Flashing homeward, again
And again, an abacus
Of pure, blurred beads,

And Williams elated
By the seeming spontaneity
Behind such control,
The pattern to its variations,
As in jazz
Or local speech.
In the bottom of the sixth,

The Yankees double their lead.
The game flows slowly through
The line-ups one last time,
As though it meant to go on forever,
The slant light falling,
It seems to him,
Like something from that painting

By Masaccio, the *Expulsion*
from Paradise, the way it bathes
The lit, attendant figures
About to step out of Eden
Into the world of time—
NEW YORK 2–CINCINNATI 0—
Of traffic and the evening news.

Death News

Visit to W.C.W. circa 1957, poets Kerouac Corso Orlovsky on sofa in living room inquired wise words, stricken Williams pointed thru window curtained on Main Street: "There's a lot of bastards out there!"

Walking at night on asphalt campus
road by the German Instructor with Glasses
W.C. Williams is dead he said in accent
under the trees in Benares; I stopped and asked
Williams is Dead? Enthusiastic and wide-eyed
under the Big Dipper. Stood on the Porch
of the International House Annex bungalow
insects buzzing round the electric light
reading the Medical obituary in *Time*.
"out among the sparrows behind the shutters"
Williams is in the Big Dipper. He isn't dead
as the many pages of words arranged thrill
with his intonations the mouths of meek kids
becoming subtle even in Bengal. Thus
there's a life moving out of his pages; Blake
also "alive" thru his experienced machines.
Were his last words anything Black out there
in the carpeted bedroom of the gabled wood house
in Rutherford? Wonder what he said,
or was there anything left in realms of speech
after the stroke & brain-thrill doom entered
his thoughts? If I pray to his soul in Bardo Thodol
he may hear the unexpected vibration of foreign mercy.
Quietly unknown for three weeks; now I saw Passaic
and Ganges one, consenting his devotion,
because he walked on the steely bank & prayed
to a Goddess in the river, that he only invented.

another Ganga-Ma. Riding on the old
rusty Holland submarine on the ground floor
Paterson Museum instead of a celestial crocodile.
Mourn O Ye Angels of the Left Wing! that the poet
of the streets is a skeleton under the pavement now
and there's no other old soul so kind and meek
and feminine jawed and him-eyed can see you
What you wanted to be among the bastards out there.

Benares, March 20, 1963

The Outernationale

One has emotions for the strangest things.
—W. C. Williams, *Kora in Hell*

So the bird's in the hand
and now what?
The penny shiny
in the dark belly of mr. piggy.
The day dawns and dawns
and may be in trouble
of actually going anywhere.
Trees migrate secretly upward. They might be saying
all we need to be here
if we would only stop
talking and listen up.
I love you, said the wood.
One sonic color into
the egregious public air.
Start from nothing and be-
long to it. I guess
the rosy and bluish streaks
move counter to the feelings
exposed beneath them.
The signal and its noise
-itsy, -ancy, -oid.
So many strangers
alive in a larynx.
So much depends on *x*
so much more
on the book in your hand.
Start from nothing
and let the sound reach you.

There is that field
in the window once again
and to write of this field
again is certainly a failure
of any inward rigor
or life. To live certainly
on the surface -ing, -ed, or
things pinging off
the metal empty core
scrolling for a perfect tune
to cue the mood
outraged or bittersweet,
vintage etc. and emptier
than the supra-empty
of the mood stabilizer
flat line -less, -let
-like, -ly. The cold parts
of the car body.
Why can't I just admit
I'm dead, have been dead
since I met me, -metry, -ality
unseen and undone
by the no time
I was raised into
out of the incubator
-obic, -etic, -istic
the stain of the world
got on me.
You see it on TV.
Everyday weather
and the everyday weatherman.
The car racing

into a slow fade.
Rain opening the next shot,
falling everywhere
around the boy falling digitally
just now as you read this.
It is always raining
in pictures, inside
this feeling of mercy
-ency, -esse
or this writing along the edge
which is of course
writing about hope
if we could only open
our hardware
to rewrite the software
down deep, the body
coming to, inside
this wooden structure
-archy, -ology, -ocracy.

Skylark, do you
have anything
to say to me?

Have you come
as a flower on the hill?

I am beside you
alive in the folds
of your parka.

Have you a single
new idea? Yes,
I carry the oldest ones.

Who will live
inside the song?

Is it only sand?
The voice of sand
-mandias, -icious, -rex.

The box is spitting electro-
magnetic lies into the room
again. I get sick and weak
just gawking to find
myself already full
of onions and laughter
-illiant, -ismus, arrogance.
I don't want to go there.
Don't want the lockdown
the bray, the cobbled headgear.
Can't it be clear? Can't it?
So often the inklings
the starter round
the jerk and huh of morning.
But the instants, the lake walks
and for a *blip* open sky
unshackling a bad history.
Nothing more personal
than headlines.
But what of the colors
in the new season sky?

It is only where
spring and death meet
-sic, -cide, -ulation.
Who says we are lacking
in courage?

The most forgotten history
is often the best. Best?
Ruined tar paper
against brick factory lots,
brick, brick,
smokestack, sky.
Even the light fades badly.
These old windows
bend the world.
I could never find
my way there and now
we are only here.
That's something
more than spectacular sunsets,
fading shafts on water.
With each one dies a world.
Or an empty casement
letting light in
bricolaged, alive for a moment
and then obfuscation
of late afternoon.
If only I knew then
what I know to be
outside my head
rain-washed and open.
Can't one stumble beyond

the cheap effects
of planet light, planet tilt
and all that google?

Once the sweet laughter
of indestructibility
cackled from my mouth.
No hiding the pain
my body was in space
and the empathy borne
of earthly gravity
earthly sentience
weighted to the bed,
the floor, the street,
the planet, -mania,
-polis, -ment.
Such cruelty comes
from lack of everything
or so I imagined,
having failed
to save anyone
from anything
in this empty house.
From this empty empty house
in first dull winter light
staring hard into spackle.
How could I save anyone
from the truly gnarly
unnecessary -osis
of a steel wind off a boulevard
rich with dog shit and perfume
carbon monoxide and subway grates

the confusion of sex and death
of childhood and decay
of sideway glances and
dinnish noises
of all things dented
and almost destroyed
amidst the once of beauty
and ankle bracelets.
The whole wide whorl
of economics charted
on a dart board
in bed sheets, -th,
-onomy, -illion, -ation.

The time to breathe
is now, there will be no time
to think but perhaps
you have no doubt.
I would like
to expose doubt itself
to open up
the mechanics of want
-ivorous, -etic, -esque, so
someone can feel it.
So someone can feel it
and break it down
inside themselves.
To rip out the gears
and belts, to empty
once and for all expectation,
the guitar sound
of young adult life

-ectric, -philia, -phyte.
The radio backdrop
speckled and moving.
The car window specked
and the sky moving.
The neighborhood
coming into view.
So the new poverty is just
like the old poverty.
The system has been upgraded
but the light, dishwater,
is mucking up the mood.
Whoever said
absolute powerlessness
corrupts absolutely?
Does it get any better?
Jeweled spots, translucent
over the windshield,
now pierced in white stinging
-hood, -holic, -hedron.
The cellular body
fuzzed out in sun,
oversaturated in Polaroid
reddish brown.
Where are we going
in the mechanical seconds
of this handheld movie,
this color that touches down?

If we could say
the world has changed,
it has changed. If we say

the world is the same
then so it is. But nothing
changes everything
and we know this.
We earn this the hard way.
Even the beloved
evolves into nothing
-unction, -iction
for all its iron and science.
A bridge expands over foliage.
The river dappled
with wind and speed
and the sensation of night.
Throw back your head
to the milky tears.
All types and shapes
of silent light.
Here the crab, the bear,
the dipper, the wheel
and the little tightnesses
that keep us wanting.
The wanting that keeps us
looking hard into the dark.
The dark we hope to unpack
and move into
that one day
we might find ourselves lit up.

Saxifrage: To the Memory of William Carlos Williams

Only the imagination is real! You declared it
time and again. But truth
is always stranger. As when, 19 years old,
punch-drunk on poetry, and Amazon at heart,
I hopped a boat to Andros.
I took you with me, Bill, a talisman
like the swiss-army knife I carried everywhere.
Everything was shut.
It was November, and tourists,
always rare at this dull spot,
were further south on the dusty beaches of Crete.
This pleased me, since I wanted
a world unspoiled, to compose itself around me.
Everything was shut. It took two hours
to find a pension that would grudgingly let me in.
The caretaker, six feet of grey malice,
showed me a room but very soon returned
with a plate of sweets, compliments of the house.
With compliments for me he lingered too long;
my Greek was poor, I thought I misunderstood.
I thought I misunderstood till he climbed into bed
and patted the sheets with a less-than-fatherly smile.
Waving my copy of your *Selected Poems*
I yelled and kicked till he fled, scratching his beard.
Chair propped against the door, I read all night.
The boat didn't leave until seven, so I walked out at five.
The town was quiet, drifting to quiet fields;
trees in second blossom, the purposeful hum of bees.
A chalky ridge looked out across the sea.
I sat there, staring down a mountain goat.
Saxifrage my flower, that splits the rock.

Red Wheel Boogie and Dog Star Night

by William Carlos Williams, as told to Charles Wright

Backyard twilight, and ooze of sun
                                        like a tissue
of eternity, daub and counter-daub,

wheel upon wheel in the circle of night.
We will never know how much depends
                                        upon this chicken,
this ritalin whirlwind glazing rusty sides
of our little bunged-up barrow,
                                  clouds and feathers, feathers and clouds.

An Exculpation

to W.C. Williams

Reed Whittemore, in his biography,
skips past your wretched poem "An Exultation,"
in which you invoke the Germans to cleanse England

of her sins against your grandmother,
with purgatorial fires lit from the skies.
It was 1941. You were fifty-eight.

The dear old woman was well gone by that time,
but T. S. Eliot was afoot in London,
directing his countrymen into the Tube.

Your words embodied some type of intent
to get someone to murder someone else.
In this case T. S. Eliot was it.

It seems you wanted him to produce a stench
of human skin and hair left smoldering,
because you did not like what he stood for.

Never mind the schoolboys to be burnt as well,
pensioners, postulants, pipe-shop proprietors,
old damsels stitching sonnets from garden paths.

When I dug your poem out of the Bound Periodicals,
I did not know whether to laugh or cry.
You sounded like a smart-ass son of a bitch

stretching back into your suburban easy chair
to seethe in spotless fury on your screened-in porch,
with a sassy little Beaujolais after lunch.

I had not come to hate poets the way you did,
enough to wish them broiled and their country charred,
while every village screamed from blazing Hell.

Fortunately, poetry makes nothing happen.
Yours was a coward's purpose to put pen to paper,
a suppuration from some morbid tissue in the mind.

The Nazis were real sons of bitches after all.
And you were no worse than many one could name.
Photographs often catch you with a scowl.

The Confessions of Doc Williams

1. (On a Trolley to the Hospital)

Doc Williams on a New York City trolley
in 1908 or so with a dead baby in a suitcase.
In charge of pediatrics, he'd found himself
in the middle of an outbreak of gastroenteritis
killing his babies like bugs.
Someone loaned an uptown mansion
for overflow patients, but stipulated *no deaths*.
When the kid died, Williams wanted it out,
fast, packed it up, took that trolley to the hospital.
What if he lost the suitcase, or it broke open,
or began to smell?—this was July.
Never again. If they died uptown, they did,
& that was that. The same with poetry.

2. (Elsa von Freytag-Loringhoven)

Hey, a real baroness who wanted to meet him.
He'd seen her sculpture that looked like chicken-guts,
& heard she dressed in purple & yellow
with a coal scuttle on her head or a tam-o'-shanter
with feathers & ice-cream spoons, or vest & kilts
with brass teaballs suspended from her nipples.
Wally Stevens saw her in the Village, applauded,
& she'd run after him, chased the portly dandy home.
Williams bailed her out of jail & fed her,
Mother of Dada, 1919, here in the New World,

baroness of black lipstick, teats dangling
empty sardine cans.
"Villiam Carlos Villiams,
I vant you," she said, jumping out of shadows
in Rutherford, vanting to giff him syph. He
resisted. She scratched him & ran. He bought
a punching bag & practiced, & when she came
for him again, dropped her with a right. Maybe
he'd played it too safe, but how mate with her?
He opted for Flossie, et al., American poetry.
The Baroness's syph blossomed away in Paris.
Her boyfriend turned the gascocks on & let her die.

3. (The Great Traditions)

I (The Fumes)

On his first spring walk in 1921, Doc
stepped in dogshit. "It brought on,"
he wrote a friend, "an irresistible desire
to study French literature."

II (Fragment from a 1935 Letter)

He wanted Walt under his bootsoles,
not "the blight of English literature
under which our cocks have all but rotted away
into each others' ass holes . . .".

4. (The Virgin)

Doc knew what to expect but still holy
shit what was it did he even like it

April evening 1927 Carnegie Hall opening to fog-
horn electric alarm bells maybe stepped-on

cats fourteen grand pianos like atonal
subway screech rushhour nervescape

imploded onstage—George Antheil's *Ballet*
Mechanique? Some got the hell out but Doc got

thinking: going home from Beethoven e.g. he'd
meditate the harmony to blot out city

insanity but Antheil counter-pointed cans
crashing unoiled metal screeching fish-

market voices scaling up the spine-
sax credenza allegro-andante not

Walt's Brooklyn ferry crossing dreaming
the sublime seagulls

"high in the air floating with motionless wings,
oscillating their bodies" but the cities'

horny musics of shears & rotgut coffee here
but clear, clarity, speaking in edges, Doc

remembering a birthblind girl patient virgin eighteen
accidentally struck on the occipital who

saw for the first time said how clear
the world was how vivid she felt cunt-quiver

chills Jesus now a jazz symphony offkey hit the buzzer
again O George my city cunt melody poetry machine!

5. (The Plums, 1935)

Purple-bruise-blue
cancer woman
with a bag of them
for solace—
what world did
the poet find him-
self in plumb
that world not

the waxy blossom
of the imagined maybe
dead ones to come she
opens her legs she
tastes good to him she
tastes good to him . . . .

6. (Mole)

Sept. 15, '42,
Doc (59 now)
burrowing under
his office for wire,
batteries, a driveshaft,
bolts, axles, any-
thing coherent,
metal, useful,
gets a snootful
of muck, finds
a cast-iron skillet
for grenades & bullets—
it's rusted here
long as his vision
of & for Paterson,
& that's long. . . .
How get it up
before it disappears
into un-
written ejaculation?

Got to get lower,
more self-enclosed, objective, the de-
notative imperative but
with teeth & claw
edges, be
that animal,
tunnel ahead
in pitch-
blende, the same

powerful pink
flippers in half-light,
lucky nose-star

burning its way
toward roots
of radium blossom.
For now, *bang,*
bang he bangs
the skillet which flakes
& clanks like
old armor or
his dull skull-bell these days *bang*
goddamnit
ring bell *bang*.

7. (Kore Again, 1945)

The bombs. *The* bombs. A week later,
that war's over. Doc,
his daughter-in-law & grandkids

home this evening when
horns begin, bells, tin cans,
shouts, whistles, firecrackers,

dogs barking, people
calling to one another, but . . .
too much suffering & death

for him to celebrate.
He sends Jinny to the movies,
stays home to watch the kids,

reads a play or two. Late,
upstairs to check,
he finds Susie

in white moonbeams
sitting up in bed.

8. (Paterson)

That Christmas Eve,
just before his father died of rectal cancer,
the helpless physician
tried to relieve him: the enema tube
wounded him. Whitman said the dead were
alive & well somewhere,

sell-out Eliot
spirited them back
into the same putrid bodies they'd decayed in, but
where *do* they go besides into herbage, brain-
ebb & flow, cloud-flow?

Not even
the new measure,
if he could find it, could stay them,
or could it, his life's theme? He would ask Paterson
as he built him. Paterson's mouth
would somehow hold
the bed of every star, & the black sea.

9. (The Verdict)

His fist clutching business letters,
Doc's father descended stairs.

"Pop, so you're not dead!" Doc shouted,
suffused with joy. But his father cut

& answered his own question:
"You know all that poetry you're writing?—

"Well, it's no good." This was the last time
Pop appeared in one of Doc's remembered dreams.

10. (The Cat)

The mid-'50s,
hot July nights in Rutherford.
Coming through the screens, driving Doc nuts,
cries of a sick cat abandoned by another of those bastards
all over out there.

Who could stand it?
A helpful friend staying with him
lured the cat into the Williams yard. Doc
sentenced it to a garbage can, poured in chloroform,
held the lid tight.

The cat went crazy,
subsided, died. The friend avoided
Doc's eyes. They dug a hole under an azure bush
on the slope facing the side street. The cat kept crying
in dead measures.

11. (The Confessions)

  1. (The Song)

From the city
    slime returned
        undersea

to the city,
    rolled onto beaches
        against bricks & boards,

tracked back by tires, shoe-leather, blood-flecks
    in feces, rat-hair, irreducible & black vomit
        sludge of all that melting,

so who was he
    to try to bury it?
        Long Island to Camden

Walt might have stood
    nonchalant at secret center
        within his saying,

letting the *Leaves* grow,
    but you'll relive/
        relieve your memory

old stroke,
    stroke, your brain-
        Pan clogging you'll

fess up to Floss
all your pussy-
willows, your muses

who last night in one body
lay on her back
her breasts

still full and upward,
you stuck your cock
between them up

to her mouth flower
& down to her moist hairy
cleft river up over belly

back again between
those nippled hills

but this time
you do not come—
that dreamy body

must have been her soul,
which must have been
your own soul,

you think, woman still
innocent despite
your deceptions,

the cotton or silk
          stockings pulled down,
                    getting/giving

head, the quickies, the affairs, decades
          of drives & quick
                    plunges, she

who was always core,
          gism & gist, the one
                    driven & ravaged would

accept anything, everything, forgive,
          at last, during this
                    awakening, you think,

so say it, rave,
          drive your wife half-
                    way to her grave who

refused to be
          buried with you,
                    but make your-

self new again, jerk your-
                    self off, let go.

2. (The Sermon)

He held on. She
held on longer.
He wanted
no religious stuff.
Spring flowers
on his coffin meant
spring flowers
on his coffin. If
there was radiance,
& there was,

then the complex love for this woman
for fifty years, the solid ground
of fatherhood, grandfatherhood,
the dedicated doctoring both of patients
& the slushy pabalum American line.
He kept yelling the one necessary thing:
stay close to speech as it is spoken—
without this: art language, insanity,
& hell. For his singular horniness,
he sought the measure, who was Kore,
the perfect virginal love
& hummingbird-tongued cocksucker. . . .

3. (Note to Doc)

Doc, it's the same country. Some of the young
stutter toward speech true to the ground, some
bumble dada-surreal in a haze growing sicker
than the Baroness or Ez. Not even the hippest angels

learned for sure what you were harping on, but
no sweat. Walt would cup your face in his hands,
kiss you, tell you for once shut up, grow up,
grow old, if need be cut off your own nuts to ripen, . . .

for words within a life, when they cohere,
sometimes flow his spinal river. Physician,
we are all soul- & body-struck
from the first solution, the new measure filtered

through a new poet's fiber, or everything is nothing, . . .
so rest in your Paterson collage-pastiche until
the next time. Every spring, the earth finds green
like a young poet finding a new little magazine,

& you in fact *are* that poet, aren't you? In Camden,
I saw you on the streets, in offices, in cabs,
in drugstores dispensing pills & prophylactics;
at his West Hills birthplace, I heard you mumbling

that the rest of us had missed the point, then
watched you run your firm masculine colter
across your notebook's page to begin again.

Liberty Brass

"the pure products"
—William Carlos Williams

I was sitting across from the rotating sign
For the Liberty Brass Turning Company

Automatic Screw Machine Products

And brooding about our fathers
Always on the make to make more money

Screw Machine Products Automatic

Tender wounded brassy unsystematic
Free American men obsessing about margins

Machine Products Automatic Screw

Selling every day of their God-dammed lives
To some Liberty Brass Turning Company

Products Automatic Screw Machine

Until they were screwed into boxes
And planted in plots paid and unpaid

Automatic Screw Machine Products

Words for Dr. Williams

Wouldst thou grace this land with song?
    Well, go yodel your head off.
But if it's poems you want, then take a town
    with mills and chimneys, oil
Slithering on the river toward the falls,
    grit in the air, a man
Just off the night shift turning, tired yet strong
    to watch the girl who hurries
Toward a timeclock step down from the bus—
    slim ankles, one,
Two, and click click click swings past. The sun
    glints on her raincoat. There's
Your muse and hero. Stick around this town
    where people speak American
And love is possible—Your stethoscope
    held to our arteries
In sickness and in health you found some places
    where our own poems grow.

For WCW

We sat in rows listening to your poems
being read at your funeral. I heard them
as you would have read them. He's not
dead, he could never die, I said to myself.
This stuff's not for funerals,
whoever you are, reading from the pulpit
in a priest's garb. You are dead wrong,
the man still is with us,
bleating his lines.

Plea for Forgiveness

The old man William Carlos Williams, who had been famous
for kindness
And for bringing to our poetry a mannerless speaking,

In the aftermath of a stroke was possessed by guilt
And began to construct for his wife the chronicle

Of his peccadilloes, and unforgivable thing, a mistake
Like all pleas for forgiveness, but he persisted

Blindly, obstinately, each day, as though in the end
It would relieve her to know the particulars

Of affairs she must have guessed and tacitly permitted,
For she encouraged his Sunday drives across the river.

His poems suggest as much; anyone can see it.
The thread, the binding of the voice, is a single hair

Spliced from the different hairs of different lovers,
And it clings to his poems, blond and dark,

Tangled and straight, and runs on beyond the page.
I carry it with me, saying, "I have found it so."

It is a world of human blossoming, after all.
But the old woman, sitting there like rust—

For her there would be no more poems of stolen
Plums, of round and firm trunks of young trees,

Only the candor of the bedpan and fouled sheets,
When there could no longer have been any hope

That he would recover, when the thing she desired
Was not his health so much as his speechlessness.

83rd Chorus

Dont call them

cat men

That lay it down
with the trumpet

The orgasm
Of the moon
and the June

I call em

   them cat things

"That's really cute,
      that un"

William
Carlos
Williams

For William Carlos Williams

When you came and you talked and you read with your
Private zest from the varicose marble
Of the podium, the lovers of literature
Paid you the tribute of their almost total
Inattention, although someone when you spoke of a pig
Did squirm, and it is only fair to report another gig-

gled. But you didn't even care. You seemed
Above remarking we were not your friends.
You hung around inside the rimmed
Circles of your heavy glasses and smiled and
So passed a lonely evening. In an hour
Of talking your honesty built you a tower.

When it was over and you sat down and the chair-
man got up and smiled and congratulated
You and shook your hand, I watched a professor
In neat bow tie and enormous tweeds, who patted
A faint praise of the sufficiently damned,
Drained spittle from his pipe, then scrammed.

Variations on a Theme by William Carlos Williams

I

I chopped down the house that you had been saving to live in next summer.
I am sorry, but it was morning, and I had nothing to do
and its wooden beams were so inviting.

II

We laughed at the hollyhocks together
and then I sprayed them with lye.
Forgive me. I simply do no know what I am doing.

III

I gave away the money that you had been saving to live on for the next ten years.
The man who asked for it was shabby
and the firm March wind on the porch was so juicy and cold.

IV

Last evening we went dancing and I broke your leg.
Forgive me. I was clumsy and
I wanted you here in the wards, where I am the doctor!

WCW on Marsden Hartley

He's a querulous bit of baggage
          more mineral than animal
                    big as a limestone cliff

and as briny   He stinks
          of months without sex
                    Over the bed a small tintype

Paris, the Quatres Arts Ball, 1912:
          In turban and garlands of jade
                    he was the new Tiresias

a watery love sheik with civet eyes
          and nose like a wedge of marble
                    I can't stand men who dress

as women he said then
          nose quivering   hips womanly
                    And wouldn't you know

in the next room
          a plaster sheet away
                    we hear it   gathering

momentum   an unmistakable
          creaking   hand over mouth
                    tooth on hand

They are newlyweds   careless
            around neighbors   ignorant
                    about plaster   He gives me

a Gauloise   scoots closer
            but I too refuse him
                    There is pigment

under his nails
            Bill   he says   *Bill!*
                    And you would have made

the most charming whore
            in New York

WCW

After prying the resisting
child's mouth open with a tablespoon
both tonsils covered with membranes

sure signs of the dreaded diptheria
after pneumonias and kidney
failures after forceps deliveries

it is hard to arrive at *this is just*
to say and *so much depends on*
to accept that they flew from the wedge

of time he wrested for his poetry
late and later at night *one occupation*
he said *complements the other*

confirmed by his son who reported
night was his time to roar
never mind that Williams's brother

returned a book of his poems
as vulgar and immoral
forgive the poet's *he was one*

of those fresh Jewish types
you want to kill on sight
overlook the crude asides

about guineas and gypsies
forgive *when the Scotch go crazy*
they are worse than a Latin

and remember him for
his revulsion against fascism
his admiration for the workingclass

women whose babies he brought forth
often after hours of harsh labor
and most of all hold fast

the freshness the unadorned
and potent plain American
speech that he saluted in his poems.

So Much Depends

Bill on the way you saw
the way your heart saw

what your eyes saw not
just the way you saw a

wheelbarrow of the falls
or the blossoms of the

shad tree or Floss in a
rose and 100 other flow-

ers your patients & the
babies and the measure

of your lines in Brueg-
hel's painting of that

dance so many things the
rest of us would never

have seen except for you.

for William Carlos Williams

Poem in the Manner of William Carlos Williams

As the rain
washes her hair
the plums red

in the bowl
on the table
with their dark

red rind wait
for her eyes
to see them

her hair still
wet still full
of suds as

three old men
watch her touch
she sees them

look at her
in the painting
of Susanna bathing

William Carlos Willams at Paterson Falls

There, your river,
the sick river,
the falls,
and a couch going
over
but first hanging
up in the outcropping tree,
upward thrusting
among the rapids.

It seems you conjured
the whole scene,
held the couch there
long enough
to study its floral pattern
like wallpaper

then you pushed it over
without thought of the iron-
clang concrete of consequence,
its abstract whirl
and definition followed
by the bottle you sucked
until age six,
the lock-out in a snowstorm
on Passaic St.,

the dollar Pop paid
you to read Darwin,
Darwin himself goes over
the falls—
gray-bearded photograph
glue-stuck to the hardback cover.

Seedy but not slummy,
every Erie RR station
smells and sounds the same
to you;
toss them all over.
Someone at the bottom
sorts them out,
sorts Pound in London
from the Hyde Park sheep
as they splash,
the Elgin marbles irrelevant
thudding into a breakwater ring.

Your English-Spanish-French-
Jewish blood spits
its own tributary falls-ward,
your American attitude
a moment of theft,
the slatterny new mother
in soiled dressing gown
as you examine her,
on house call rounds,

her child, say all's well,
and you will take
one of the pink curlers
from her dirty brown hair.
It goes over the falls,
beneath the whirl and rush,
eddying unseen
beneath modern poetry,
its books, their
explication de texte
all gone to you, you there
at river's edge,
thinking of that mother
and the other patients
you lusted after,
thinking of the woman
who called that morning
as you wrote a poem.
You said, "Your child
swallowed a mouse?
Get her to swallow
a cat!"
You hung up the phone
so hard its bell
rang and rang
in your ears,
still rings around you,
you, who in years,
hear Flossie
read Marjorie Kinnan Rawlings
to you, blind.

Williams: An Essay

His theme
over and over:

the twang of plucked
catgut
from which struggles
music,

the tufted swampgrass
quicksilvering
dank meadows,

a baby's resolute fury—metaphysic
of appetite and tension.

Not
the bald image, but always—
undulant, elusive, beyond reach
of any dull
staring eye-lodged

among the words, beneath
the skin of image: nerves,

muscles, rivers
of urgent blood, a mind

secret, disciplined, generous and
unfathomable.
Over

and over,
his theme
                    hid itself and
smilingly reappeared.

                                        He loved
persistence—but it must
be linked to invention: landing
backwards, facing
into the wind's teeth,
                                        to please him.

He loved
the lotus cup, fragrant
upon the swaying water, loved

the wily mud
pressing swart riches into its roots,

and the long stem of connection.

Making It Work

3-foot blue cannisters of nitro
along a conveyor belt, slow fish
speaking the language of silence.
On the roof, I in my respirator
patching the asbestos gas lines
as big around as the thick waist
of an oak tree. "These here are
the veins of the place, stuff
inside's the blood." We work in rain,
heat, snow, sleet. First warm
spring winds up from Ohio, I
pause at the top of the ladder
to take in the wide world reaching
downriver and beyond. Sunlight
dumped on standing and moving
lines of freight cars, new fields
of bright weeds blowing, scoured
valleys, false mountains of coke
and slag. At the ends of sight
a rolling mass of clouds as dark
as money brings the weather in.

When People First Said I Must Have Been Influenced by William Carlos Williams

I hadn't even read him though I knew about one
of his favorite painters. I guess I knew him thru
poems I loved. Paul Blackburn especially.
Poets whose poems were connected to breath,
were thinking in motion. Of course I had no idea
they read William Carlos Williams years before.
I probably avoided meeting him, being doctor
phobic. Had I known he worked harder at being
a writer than a physician I wouldn't have avoided
him. He knew my good friend Vincent Millay.
After studying 5 syllable words in a blue WORD
WEALTH book to score high on the SAT exam,
drowning in 16th and 17th century poetry in college,
I wanted words that caught the way people thought
and spoke. It was why I picked Wyatt for a PhD
dissertation. There was a lot about Williams I
didn't know before we met, a lot we had in common:
doing theater with a passion and getting in trouble
for using real people's names. We both were fascinated
with Paris. Though I'd been at Yaddo artists' colony,
I never knew he had too. And both of us fought
depression. I always tell my students to use their senses
and by the time WC and I met, I was enthralled
not only by the breathless rush in his poems but
the way his poems make people see "no ideas
but in things." Green bed quilts, flowers, lavender and
yellow, a red wheel barrow glazed with rain water.
No morals. He was accessible, not always a thing critics
like or fad writers lately it seems. And he was accessible

as a person. Hard to believe I waited so long to try to meet. He taught me so much. But I had a little bit of trivia that amused him about Stieglitz' lost work and how an unfaithful boyfriend who was fooling around with a real estate agent, a drunk with two blond babies and a piano tuning husband who was going deaf fast enough not to hear them plotting to buy a house she showed with a closet of Stieglitz negatives but only if they could be sure they were real. Williams looked wide eyed as I told him how the two thought they were so smart, smuggled the photographs out, brought them to the Whitney and to *Aperture Magazine*, how they got bids and estimates, played museums against each other, were counting their big bucks until they hit a snag, were pretty much caught doing some thing not quite legal. Sure, the photographs were real and the appraisal said it but the date for buying the house came later—at least a misdemeanor or more to take what is not yours out. So their great dreams vanished and they settled for a quick lower private sale. For years I wish I'd just slid one photograph, a small one with a little boy just sitting, out and put it in my bag. But I didn't. I was too jealous of what I knew was going on. Williams was fascinated with my story. I told him some art teacher somewhere had also looked at the house and had a glimpse of the Stieglitz gems so my boyfriend and that woman were cooked. I still have negatives of photographs of the photographs. It's not like they are worth anything but I made another copy of them for WC. He said what he liked about them was the earthiness, the ordinary, normal people doing normal things. He had a painter's eye. I do wish I'd taken some of the original photographs, (they disappeared for years and then began to be shown) so I could have given the doctor one of them.

William Carlos Williams

Who loved more? William Carlos Williams,
in collegiate black slacks, gabardine coat,
and loafers polished like rosewood on yachts,
straying stonefoot through his town-end garden,
man and flower seedy with three autumn strokes,
his brown, horned eyes enlarged, an ant's, through glasses;
his Mother, stonedeaf, her face a wizened talon,
her hair the burnt-out ash of lush Puerto Rican grass;
her black, blind, bituminous eye inquisitorial.
"Mama," he says, "which would you rather see here,
me or two blondes?" Then later, "The old bitch
is over a hundred, I'll kick off tomorrow."
He said, "I am sixty-seven, and more
attractive to girls than when I was seventeen."

Eka Pada Rajakapotasana: One Legged King Pigeon Pose

William Carlos Williams
wrote poems
on a notebook
small enough to fit
in his breast pocket
on his medical rounds.

The body writes stories
small enough to fit
in the tiniest cell.
Every centimeter
has a different beginning
and end.
Day by day
the gap between
beginning and end
thigh and floor
heel and head
closes up,
the narrative writ large
on each small movement.

Start small and the world expands
as Goethe said, but start anyway.
In beginnings
there is the magic
of *yes*.

The Young Doctor (1916)

He smiles and nods
as he drives by
thinking perhaps soon
she will be pregnant
coming to me
but he's wrong.
He sees a long line
of pregnant women
packed like fish
in a net bursting out
the seams of their dresses.
Ah. Give me a cup
of tea and a back rub.
Blood slime cupids cherubs, no thanks.
Give me trees losing their leaves.
I'm okay. I pay the ice man
and he brings ice
into the dark house
inserts the block of it
into the icebox
a dark womb of art,
while church bells dong dong
scaring the mice.
"Then again" as the fish man's nag
comes towing an old wagon
of trout, I turn about
to see who's driving by
and it's he, no lazy he,
I'm beginning to think

driving out of his way
maybe at least a mile
just to smile at me.
But no, that's crazy.
Against distant thunder
I watch my trout of many blues
being wrapped in trodden newspaper
and blundered by shaky hands.
And I understand.

Elegy for William Carlos Williams on the Eve of His 125th Birthday

A chic Italian restaurant here on Rutherford's
Park Avenue. On the corner across the street:
your home, sold to strangers. All those bright
flowers you & Flossie tended to in your back yard

gone. A piece of still-warm bread & a bottle of
Chianti I had to bring myself. It's a dry town still,
where the mythy gods of wine stay suspect, Bill.
A blue flame gutters my lonely table. I ask

the waitress, first name Cora, who's worked here
the past four years, if she's ever heard of you.
A poet. You know, one of those. Spent his whole life
here in this godforsaken Jersey suburb long before

the stadium came to nest in the purple cattailed
meadows. Coaxed three thousand kids into this new
world naked, making endless calls on these same
ramshackle four-square rooms, leaving poems

at every railroad crossing, as he netted isolate flecks
of images from the sick, majestic river that runs
through town, heading for the black Atlantic
to be lost. "A poet, huh?," she says, in that

distinctive twang my poor mother had in life.
"Right here in this ol' town. Well, I'll be damned."
As we all are, don't you know, with our broken
cries and words. Again the dark descends

as she leaves me to myself. Except for the bells,
You were never one for Catholic rituals, old friend,
but let me ring one in tonight. A crust of bread
here in my left hand and a glass of dago red

here in my right, which now I lift to you,
listening as you taught me with the one good ear
I've left for the river's sad and distant music riffing
those jagged Jersey sounds you loved so well.

From a Window

The shadow does not move.
—William Carlos Williams

i.

Day ascends into day,
and last night's
vocabulary
is lost.

Through the bone
of a stutter

lodged in my throat,
to somehow say
what wants to be said.

Say it.

Black moth
wrecked
against glass.

Cactus aglow
on a narrow ledge.

ii.

Between
a bulk of clouds

broken
over dawn

blackbirds
disperse.

Page
as white
as the sun.

iii.

This year's
        first few
rhododendrons

        hover above
purple and orange
        flowers I

can't find
        in the field guide.

iv.

Paint can
        half-sunk
in dried mud

        full of yesterday's
                rain.

v.

Lit amber by
back door light

a skunk prowls
bramble's edge

—blackberry vines
and dandelions

bunched alongside
the garage—

into alley's black
spilling moths.

vi.

Weeds after
days of rain
and fog
curve

from one end
of the sidewalk
to the other

above snails crushed
while walking home
last night
drunk in the dark.

vii.

In vines'

leaves
latticed over
the sunk shed roof

gnats or bees
—both—blur.

viii.

Over the window
            cobwebs
embody a breeze
            neither of us feel.

ix.

Gibbous moon
splinters

past bare
fuchsia branches

and my face
cast

on lamp-glared
glass.

x.

Dawn skims the blinds
into a shape   shadows

—children, traffic, pigeons
cut across—

What's left of the dream:
a hole in my head

the dreamed words
draw through and decompose.

xi.

The hills
aligned

with clouds
aligned

with the
windowsill

levitate.

On Reading "Days and Nights" by Kenneth Koch

When Kenneth Koch wrote "William Carlos Williams"
As an end word for a sestina, and "grass"
As another, maybe he was getting sleepy
Or just plain having fun. When I came to "hog snout,"
I knew that was where I'd run out of breath
In my attempt to finish his sestina–what a dream

That would be! Did Kenneth Koch dream
Anyone would even bother? Now, William Carlos Williams,
Did he ever spend precious time and breath
On a sestina, over in N.J., with the grass
To mow, *Paterson* to write, receiving pickled hog snout
In return for medical treatment and never getting sleepy?

I've just been thinking how it's X-mas that makes me sleepy–
All those presents and people, certainly no dream
Of sugar plums! And there's always the hog snout,
I mean *turkey* to roast. Me, with William Carlos Williams'
Collected Poems, lying on the sunny grass
Of some warmer clime, with just a breath

Of jasmine in the air – now that would be worth the breath
Of an after-dinner call home to all those sleepy
Relatives, who live where it's too dry for green grass,
Who dye their hair lavender or pink and still dream
Of Valentino, but who wouldn't know William Carlos Williams
From a pump handle, a box or chocolates or a hog snout.

Come to think of it, Aunt Elfrieda tacked a hog snout
Up on her wall and no amount of loving, familial breath
Could convince her it wasn't a wild boar. William Carlos Williams
Would have understood her (whereas I just get sleepy
Or else lose my patience) as part of the poet's dream
To celebrate each and every blade of grass

In the field, no matter how old or odd the grass.
He would have understood Aunt Elfrieda's hog snout
Cum wild boar and her breast that had harbored a dream
Of cinematic dimensions, her peanut butter breath,
Her flat feet scuffing to the bathroom when she was sleepy
As if he'd been her one true love, this William Carlos Williams.

Adoration of that hog snout on Aunt Elfrieda's breath,
The colors of her withered dream in that sad, sleepy
Place with no grass: a poem, between patients, for WCW.

From the Cutting-Room Floor

Thanks. Dr. Williams, my throat feels better already.
ANY TIME. I WASN'T IN THE AUDIENCE
WHEN YOU READ YR OPUS Oh dear— PLEASE DE NADA!
NEITHER WAS WHITMAN. WE SULKED IN OUR TENTS:
'BILL, I MADE DO WITH A DOORWAY IF IT HAD A
LILAC OR A HANDSOME LAD IN IT,
YOU WITH A SMALL TOWN & BABIES. GUESS WE MISSED
THE TRAIN?' But you were . . . America! LAND OF THE FREE
SAMPLE, HOME OF THE (GRADE B) RAVE. FADS, FADS:
WHAT HAPPENED TO THE BEATNIKS? KEROUAC
WAS HERE, MADE A BRIEF TRUCKER'S STOP Then? BACK.
WHAT WOULD HAVE KEPT HIM? I ENVIED BODENHEIM
HIS HOUR OF FAME. WHERE'S OLD MAX NOW? A BLACK
CANE WORKER IN CUBA. *Your* star, though, would seem
Fixed in our skies. YOU KNOW WHY? WHITMAN. 'BY GOD
(HE SAID) BILL STAYS OR I GO BACK WITH HIM!'
Good for you both! I MISS LIFE. LIFE WAS GOOD.
Well, can't we always botch our lives in order
Just to be born again, time after time?
NOT IF THE STAR CHUGS OFF & LEAVES ITS BOARDER.

By Defective Means

There is no direction. Whither?
—William Carlos Williams, *Paterson*

Do you know this part of Paterson?
—Allen Ginsberg to WCW in *Paterson*

I had planned to hit Paterson while it was still dark.
Would the things still be things, thought thought?

My dashboard—
                              generalizing the particular

          dust, trash, the interior
                                        —glowing green

And nothing beyond the green
          glow, thought

Smearing across NJ like a firefly,
          barreling

                                        to Paterson.

But not before the sun got there first
                              (Too sentimental, pristine)
before the city remembers the psychosis
a thousand silky automatons
have cocooned its brain in.
Before it could open its mouth,
before the earth and air chatter convulsing
before I could see it as just another place,

the morning belonged to the sun.
No sign of Williams except
DOCTOR'S CAVE LOUNGE: GO GO GIRLS
(if that counts)
and a piece of ancient extant poetry
which I can't write down, because
I took all my pens out of my pocket
so they wouldn't explode while sleeping
in the back seat of my Buick in PA.

—You have pens?
—I have pencils.
—Sharpened?
—These kind.
—Are there any diners for breakfast?
—I have sandwich.
—I mean sit down.
—There's Burger King over there.

I get pencil and ride, now on bicycle, back to the ancient words:

PATERSON SILK MACHINERY EXCHANGE
LOOMS WARPERS WINDERS QUILLERS COPPERS
JACQUARDS & SUPPLIES

The generations that must have puzzled
over this poem!

Especially because the Q in JACQUARD—

hardest, most lost!

rarest word!—

was the letter most eroded.

Stairs to an overlook.
Shell of a bandshell.
Glass like seashells
and graffiti.

Quick shuttering
of Super 8.

The cataract of the falls appears
like a stereoscope slide in a restaurant dumpster.

The Krishnas espied from afar
turn out to be convicts in bright orange jumpers.

—Enlightened!

Before the mind starts, again
before recognition discombobulates
before anyone thinks of pulling back
corsages, factories, soda fountains
out of the void, the bloody mess
of nostalgia, Lou Costello appears,
bronzed.

Not by Hollywood sun,
but by Bronze itself,

to remind us
"Who's On First?"
was a better poem
than Paterson,
and that
is language for you

its bronze cheer.

Later I learn that Super 8 has just been
discontinued, so this is my last roll,
rolling brief seconds of the city up,
unsure if the meter is correct (has the roll
finished?) both rushing to the end and
making a deliberate effort to capture what counts.

It could be that the door has opened,
and the meter reset, and the ending expired long ago.

For W. C. Williams

In all the deepest thrusting
points of my knowledge
                                        bearing
the weight on them of
                                        those sharpest moments on which
everything depended—
                                        there you spoke (them
words jutting out of
those crevices bursting
                                        open where the center is: there
It was said,   as I have longed to
say it,   do it
                    & continue
from there,   from the hundreds of
theres   leading
into tangents
                              which when
you speak them,   cease to
be tangents: are center
                                        And the breaks,
                                        the pauses,
parentheses, diminuendos,
                                             accelerandos
                                                                 you have dared
accomplish them
                              & I tremble over them in fierceness
of recognition
                              now I have found you at last
                                                                    whose hand I can

take in trustfulness
closest of
those who have fathered me, whom
in your lifetime
I did not come to see,   out of
diffidence that has cursed & almost damned me
With what certainty you say your say—as I would
write those words on the skin of
my body—tattoo my chest with them,   so
I said at dinner less than
3 nights ago
I rise to
your bait,
I am your fish
swimming
in the darkest waters of
our time,
in this wastage,
this ugliness,
corruption
of our cities,
blurring of
distinctions,
breakdown of
language as of everything for which there must be
ears   to listen to more than
poundings only,
eyes to see
more than gloss, shine, glitter
to see
sharply
& behind things

To your word
I rise up saying "thoughts alight & scatter"
They begin!
"the perfections are sharpened"
I bow to you,
I, like you, having
"only of late, late!
begun to know, to
know clearly (as through clear ice)
whence I draw my breath
or how to employ it clearly—if not well—"
Hearing today in
this Elizabethan garden of Oxfordshire
the strong clarity
of bird-speech
as you heard
"the red-breast . . . clearly!"
the harsh song of
the Icterine Warbler recalling
"both the Nightingale's and
the Marsh Warbler's" song,
though "the jumble of notes each repeated . . . includes both
musical and discordant ones",
it rings out
in defiance, a ring of energy pitted
against the world,
the late, green-leaved,
half-greeting, half-wet, sometimes shining
world
Rising, I bow to you, searcher,
dealer in truth, refusing
"the non-purveyors"

refusing
to pretend direction. Whither? I
cannot say, I cannot say
more than now . . . watching—
colder than stone.
alone
in a wind that does not move the others—
knowing
"There is no recurrence. The past is dead."
I climb in the tracks you made,
in your despair,
humility—where you split the rocks & tore them
with your fingers,
where your hands were torn
open.
With what certainty
& despite
the "divisions . . . imbalances" despite "the vague.
the particular no less vague" the knowledge of
"terrible things"
with what certainty
you say your say
though "there has been again & again
a terrible postponement"
Barely clinging
to the edge of a plank,
dragged on my knees
in the wake of an iron chariot,   I knew
the numbed attempts at speech,
blind efforts
of touching,   the inarticulate cries, the brushing past of
voices, the deaf singing, years of spasmodic

scribbling,
but warmed by your brooding fire,
made over
by your patience,   impatience,   despair,
with
nothing lost, nothing left-out,
nothing
uncared for.
True father of my spirit
I acknowledge you,
my joy in you
public & secret both—knowing what must be
torn away, dislodged, pulled down,
so invention
can begin.
Later than most I come
to you,
& needing to expiate
the tardiness, as all my other tardinesses in
self-awareness.
Streams, water, the loosing
of tides & currents,
winds shaping
the surface of water into differing
crests,   the dive & texture
of waves,
have held me, as
they have given you images of
the movements of gathering thoughts or
thought scattered
For me, more often
standing at the edge of the sea, watching

what moves stealthily off the horizon
            & deeply, invisibly
almost begins a slow stride, a dance in
several directions at once
        for me the sea is
catharsis, a scouring, a stripping away of extraneous elements
a cleansing, a rebirth.
       The sea for you is
murder "where the day drowns"
          "in whom the dead,
enwombed again cry out to us to return"
            For me it is
touching the source again,
         rubbing my body
against the seeds of beginning,
         core of renewal
   I must speak of fire as you do—for me,
breakdown of communication & the "secret joy" of
the others "a defiance of authority . . . So be it."
    I beg to be taught
         & even by indirection
your shadow lengthening toward me,
            —of this, make it of *this*.

This Is the Time for Which We Have Been Waiting

Dear Jim,

I #fnally got your letter enclosing Your letter enclocussing your letter which was so ompportant foe me, thannkouk yuon very much. In time This fainful bsiness will will soonfeul will soon Be onert.Tnany anany goodness. If S lossiee eii Wyyonor wy sinfsignature.

I hope I hope I make it.

Bill

The first snowfall brings chaos.
First the horizon disappears, then
you disappear. When

William Carlos Williams suffered his first stroke
he was 68 years old, in 1951. His second,
the following year. The man loved

our American speech. Vulgar & graceless
as oversized boots he loved it. The pimply-
faced girl he loved. Forms inside things gnarly

to the touch. Smokestacks, mustard weed.
The steely river filling with acid & sparrows
picking in the dirt, like Death. Yet

still just sparrows. Beauty of marigolds,
& fried oysters. Beauty of spiderwebs,
Brueghel's hunters in the snow. Except

maybe what the poet saw & heard
was in his own head! Maybe in Rutherford,
N.J. there was nothing. Maybe

he was in despair, fierce lover
of women & adulterer & this morning waking to discover
someone has dressed him in an old man's underwear—

gunmetal-gray, woollen-itchy, soiled cuffs
at bony wrists & ankles & the crotch unsnapped.
Opens his mouth to curse

& words choke like phlegm. A doctor doesn't expect
to die like the rest of us . . . Waking in the sun
in Flossie's garden back of the yellow house

the terror strikes him maybe he's dreamt it all?—male
hands lifting a thrashing bloody infant
from between female thighs, &

ironweed along the railroad embankment
tough enough to thrive in cinders, &
there he's laughing typing on the old manual

words leaping astonished out of the mute keyboard, keys
so worn you can't read the letters. And
those clouds—

Clouds I've been noticing this morning, too.
Diesel-dirtied, broken & yet dignified in motion
moving from west to east effortless above the pines

in this New Jersey smudged sky. In March 1963
the final stroke. "Died in his sleep." Eyes
moving restlessly down the naked body.

On a gurney? Since when? The shock of it, his young
male body restored. Svelte dark down of the chest,
groin & soft stirring penis. Winter-pale

haunches, muscles hard as bone. Lifts
his head. Where? Christ he's alert, he's curious—
ready to begin it all again—

This is the time for which we have been waiting.

Note: The letter from William Carlos Williams to his friend and editor James Laughlin was written sometime shortly prior to June 1962 when Williams's last book, *Pictures From Brueghel and Other Poems*, was published.

To a Poet

I am sober and industrious
and would be plain and plainer
for a little while
                                until my rococo
self is more assured of its
distinction.
                        So you do not like
my new verses, written in the
pages of Russian novels while I do
not brood over an orderly
childhood?
                        You are angry
because I see the white-haired
genius of the painter more beautiful
than the stammering vivacity

                                                of
your temperament. And yes,
it becomes more and more a matter
of black and white between us

and when the doctor comes to
me he says "No things but in ideas"
or it is overheard
                                in the public
square, not that I am off my couch.

Red Mallows

for WCW

red mallows, the language blooming
like those flowers, August,
in my garden this morning, he
said, the first time this year

    as flowers do

declaring the accidence
not by the law, not by nature
(admitting her regularity,
and the need for relations)
but by what troubles discourse:

    that it is I
    who speaks

Beauty—what others love in us—
is not responsible to us, she
said, and thereby, also,
raised the question:

    form
    descends

And the inhabitation
—the eyes, and the ears,
responsible agents, the places
they have to nose into, nose
about—it is they

who also
come up

We Mark the Centennial of William Carlos Williams' Birth Observing a New Hampshire Patriot

yes i know a
lot depends on
the white house with
its pink shutters
even without
rain falling

the pink flowers
tended so carefully
by the pink old lady
in a pink combo pink
shorts pink polo pink
tennies

this evening
we watch her after
she waters the flowers

she moves the
american flag from
its holder on the wall

that holder which
sends it soaring
each day above
those pink flowers
red white and blue

she puts the flag
in the partial cover
of the open porch
leaning it against wall

then she carefully
dries her hands
with it

A Critical Glance at William Carlos Williams' Poem "The Dance"

In Williams' famous poem about The Kermess,
the lines go round, they go round, and
around line 3 music pitches in for a fling and the
reader hears bugle, bagpipes and fiddles,
when slightly tipsy dancers, amorous and thick,
leap into the fray, beer sloshing, feet pounding
bodies whirling until the reader is thrown off-
balance by one gerund after another, nouns
rolling about in loose patches of poetry, such
delight, such rollicking frolicking souls as images
dance in Williams' famous poem about The
Kermess.

Excerpt from "Canto LXXVIII" (from *The Pisan Cantos*)

. . . and as for the solidity of the white oxen in all this
          perhaps only Dr Williams (Bill Carlos)
                    will understand its importance,
          its benediction. He wd/ have put in the cart.
The shadow of the tent's peak treads on its corner peg
marking the hour. The moon split, no cloud nearer than Lucca.
In the spring and autumn
   In "The Spring and Autumn"
                              there
                              are
                              no
                            righteous
                              wars

For Doctor WCW

Williams' courtly *Greeny Asphodel*
shows love triumphant
and poetry

triumphant, over the bomb
the blade, bullet, even the sting
of the quotidian bee.

Williams, the actual physician
in the actual thousand rooms
witness to the actual expirations

of his Jersey neighbors
knew disease as the actual depletion
and particular pain of the flesh.

Williams—who knew poetry cures
no actual illness
in the external world,

said if he were to write
in a larger way than
of the birds and flowers,

rather to write of those close
about him in all
the actual rooms—

would return from his rounds
in the declining days
to Flossie

his wife upon whom
so much
depended.

Violets in a Pewter Vase

for Lockie

As if they were a crowd of pilgrims
    singing in the rain,
each drop complected like the globe
    set in a silver frame,

their music rises from an earth
    that will not stay in tune
so brittle are its longitudes
    and so pale its moon.

A Letter to William Carlos Williams

Dear Bill,

When I search the past for you,
Sometimes I think you are like
St. Francis, whose flesh went out
Like a happy cloud from him,
And merged with every lover—
Donkeys, flowers, lepers, suns—
But I think you are more like
Brother Juniper, who suffered
All indignities and glories
Laughing like a gentle fool.
You're in the *Fioretti*
Somewhere, for you're a fool, Bill,
Like the Fool in Yeats, the term
Of all wisdom and beauty.
It's you, stands over against
Helen in all her wisdom,
Solomon in all his glory.

Remember years ago, when
I told you you were the first
Great Franciscan poet since
The Middle Ages? I disturbed
The even tenor of dinner.
Your wife thought I was crazy.
It's true, though. And you're "pure," too,
A real classic, though not loud
About it—a whole lot like
The girls of the Anthology.

Not like strident Sappho, who
For all her grandeur, must have
Had endometriosis,
But like Anyte, who says
Just enough, softly, for all
The thousands of years to remember.

It's a wonderful quiet
You have, a way of keeping
Still about the world, and its
Dirty rivers, and garbage cans,
Red wheelbarrows glazed with rain,
Cold plums stolen from the icebox,
And Queen Anne's lace, and day's eyes,
And leaf buds bursting over
Muddy roads, and splotched bellies
With babies in them, and Cortes
And Malinche on the bloody
Causeway, the death of the flower world.

Nowadays, when the press reels
With chatterboxes, you keep still,
Each year a sheaf of stillness,
Poems that have nothing to say,
Like the stillness of George Fox,
Sitting still under the cloud
Of all the world's temptation,
By the fire, in the kitchen,
In the Vale of Beavor. And
The archetype, the silence
Of Christ, when he paused a long
Time and then said, "Thou sayest it."

Now in a recent poem you say,
"I who am about to die."
Maybe this is just a tag
From the classics, but it sends
A shudder over me. Where
Do you get that stuff, Williams?
Look at here. The day will come
When a young woman will walk
By the lucid Williams River,
Where it flows through an idyllic
News from Nowhere sort of landscape,
And she will say to her children,
"Isn't it beautiful? It
Is named after a man who
Walked here once when it was called
The Passaic, and was filthy
With the poisonous excrements
Of sick men and factories.
He was a great man. He knew
It was beautiful then, although
Nobody else did, back there
In the Dark Ages. And the
Beautiful river he saw
Still flows in his veins, as it
Does in ours, and flows in our eyes,
And flows in time, and makes us
Part of it, and part of him.
That, children, is what is called
A sacramental relationship.
And that is what a poet
Is, children, one who creates
Sacramental relationships
That last always."
With love and admiration,
Kenneth Rexroth.

W.C.W.—In Memoriam

I wasn't there the evening
Ezra read the poem he just scribbled
on the back of some other writer's dust jacket.
Your father was listening and wondering
what the words could mean; while you
felt the anguish of having to be
decent and frank at the same time.

Living with poetry then
was very much like living in sin.

Fragment

Fittingly
"Fragment" is the first whole poem
(on p. 23 of *Pictures from Brueghel*
and Other Poems by William Carlos Williams)
that remains intact.

I found the remains this morning
in a pine grove out back, half-hidden
by needles and winter leaves.

Was it mice chewed
the torn white pages
unglued and wedded to earth by snow—

black words on white paper
imprinted and numbered page by page
the cover spattered and torn

in pieces, leavings of insects and God-knows-what-else
lay or burrowed into this text,
looking for protection Williams

didn't factor in. In "Fragment"
he writes

as for him who
finds fault
may silliness

and sorrow
overtake him
when you wrote

you did not
know
the power of

your words

Did he understand the power
of his own to attract—

to be carried somehow from my writing house
to this grove by unseen
hand—or claw on paw
of a heaving creature
longing for what it couldn't name?

But Williams could
in the section and other poems,
growing lichen and pressed together
in a damp community of words.

I decided the creature was larger than mouse—
the arc of its bite, three quarters of an inch
with a delicate edge as of pinking shears
small shears to be found in a house
built by a writer of children's books
and piercing pp. 23 through 45,

47 reduced to one tooth mark
just on the edge, making it less than perfect.

But who can speak of perfection now?

Spots of mold purplish to gray
like those on the forehead of late middle age
mottle the upper half of 47.

Only the start of part III, To all the girls
of all ages
who walk up and down on

the streets of this town
silent or gabbing
putting—

only this is without blemish.
"Perpetuum Mobile," Williams called it
and well he might have
his living text resurrected from soil

no less than Christ, giving life
(perpetuum mobile) not only to girls
but to the whale above in "Histology,"
to the sumac in "Exercise . . ." that died,
as well as to the unnamed creature
who hauled it away.

And I? I found the text
missing since fall.
I've brought it into my house
to translate the signs.

Mullens

My mother points her cane
at a flower nearly hidden
by the lilies. She prods the
deep-pink blossom, saying
I can't recall the name; then
a few minutes later, she speaks
again—*I think we called them*
mullens—and I say, *Yes, that's it,*
pleased that she remembers, that we
can agree, but she's already
changed her mind or forgotten—
she's moved on
to the edge of the garden.

And then here it is again,
cropping up on this late
August afternoon
in a poem called "Chloe,"
by Williams—"the magenta
flower / of the / moth-mullen"—
and I dog-ear the page
to show her. This time I'll call
her back—I'll remind her
that a flower's name is
a kind of a song, and that
poetry, like love, can
reinvent us.

For WCW

Now they are trying to make you
The genital thug, leader
Of the new black shirts—
Masculinity over all!
I remember you after the stroke
(Which stroke? I don't remember which stroke.)
Afraid to be left by Flossie
In a hotel lobby, crying out
To her not to leave you
For a minute. Cracked open
And nothing but womanish milk
In the hole. Only a year
Before that we were banging
On the door for a girl to open,
To both of us. Cracked,
Broken. Fear
Slaughtering the brightness
Of your face, stroke and
Counterstroke, repeated and
Repeated, for anyone to see.
And now, grandmotherly,
You stare from the cover
Of your selected poems—
The only face you could compose
In the end. As if having
Written of love better than any poet
Of our time, you stepped over
To that side for peace.
What valleys, William, to retrace
In memory, after the masculine mountains,
What long and splendid valleys.

From the Desk of William Carlos Williams: Notes Toward a Speech in Three Parts

I.

Thrown from the chalky cliffs
of death: another birth,   and another,
everyone for the moment striving
and well, doing their jobs, or doing
nothing, stung deadpan, waiting,
plopped between one world and some stark
other, the dazed infant inching
up mother's belly, stuck
between that loved breast
and the softly spasming cord.

II.

Drops down, another dusk. Unless
the cloudless sky, the scant flight
of stars. Defeat after such dull
defeat. We are beset
by privilege and woe. We are
divided but no different.
Who will save us? Who will say
all's decided, that, at last,
all's decidedly swell?

III.

Beware the experiment found ingrowing
on the shelf. What is it but life
in want of greater means?

What is it but the crutch of self-love
searching for a wafer-thin faith?
Propped in a deadening appetite
of ease, I recall the quick comedy
of a demonstrating woman
(headstrong. . . underfoot)
caught by local news, surrounded
by a blue line of courtesy.
To the camera, that escorting cop:
"Your heroes all are dead.
Or should be."

—The poem is an anagram of W. C. Williams's "Spring and All" and "This Is Just to Say."

For William Carlos Williams

July 1960

queen-ann's-lace
always in the wind

then holds the
summer stillness

a child white
lace upon lace

almost to her eyes
spreads her hand

to encompass
the flower

the picked weeds
fall in a

white
powder

each needle-
tube

that has held and
fed

the minutest sub-
traction of

flower
releases a

dry
seed

except the
dark

flower still
soft

purple
at the center

A Red Wheelbarrow

Rest and look at this goddamned wheelbarrow. Whatever
It is. Dogs and crocodiles, sunlamps. Not
For their significance.
For their significance. For being human
The signs escape you. You, who aren't very bright
Are a signal for them. Not,
I mean, the dogs and crocodiles, sunlamps. Not
Their significance.

Understanding Poetry, by William Carlos Williams and Wallace Stevens

The jar on a mountain, the tree that thinks
for the rest, these return when they seem to begin.
They realize out of the earth, brought back
by the sun and stirred by the wind for a storm.

And the *you* that thinks—where can it find
a song in the branches?—feel the becoming?
A formula that you carry around
has the universe like a spring inside.

From anyone, from a tree, a hill,
everything else may arrive. It has
a little box with a sign on top:
"Open on your birthday. The inside is yours."

What waits, the old discoverers found,
is often disguised. It sleeps in the sun,
or it escapes, too small to see.
But it, or lack of it, can kill a man.

Nuances of a Theme by Williams

It's a strange courage
you give me, ancient star:

Shine alone in the sunrise
toward which you lend no part!

I

Shine alone, shine nakedly, shine like bronze
that reflects neither my face nor any inner part
of my being, shine like fire, that mirrors nothing.

II

Lend no part to any humanity that suffuses
you in its own light.
Be not chimera of morning,
Half-man, half-star.
Be not an intelligence,
Like a widow's bird
Or an old horse.

Getting to Sleep in New Jersey

Not twenty miles from where I work,
William Williams wrote after dark,

after the last baby was caught,
knowing that what he really ought

to do was sleep. Rutherford slept,
while all night William Williams kept

scratching at his prescription pad,
dissecting the good lines from the bad.

He tested the general question whether
feet or butt or head-first ever

determines as well the length of labor
of a poem. His work is over:

bones and guts and red wheelbarrows;
the loneliness and all the errors

a heart can make the other end
of a stethoscope. Outside, the wind

corners the house with a long crow.
Silently, his contagious snow

covers the banks of the Passaic River,
where he walked once, full of fever,

tracking his solitary way
back to his office and the white day,

a peculiar kind of bright-eyed bird,
hungry for morning and the perfect word.

Turning

Our dreams have been assaulted
by a memory that will not
sleep.
—William Carlos Williams

I.
Leaving is only possible with the intention
of returning; otherwise, the loss seems unbearable.
We numb the memories of our old lands,
equivocate the voice of a child inside us calling, *where*
is my mother, where
is my father?

II.
In humid June, my young sister-in-law
and I go for a walk on the gravel road.
Black dogs come after us,
barking with deep red inside their mouths.
Their sharp teeth deceive our eyes. We
believe their power and anger, but are they afraid
of our voices?
We make a detour of five miles, never turn
around to face the dogs' yellow fear.

III.
In August, my young sister-in-law has a terrible headache
during her older sister's wedding. She is pale as a river
breaks, flooding her inside.
My husband walks on a busy street in a strange city to look
for some medicine for her. The young girl's suffering
and his compassion tangle into a rope, which pull him

far. Will he know when
to turn around? Or will he be lost
in his compassion, inside her river?

IV.

It is always the same dream. After a dinner of deep-fried oysters,
I wash rice bowls and round
dishes for my family. The kitchen is on fire
with the smell of grease and sweat.
I drain the oily water; my mother
washes soybeans behind me
by the ashen wall. I am no more
than this wooden bowl full of beans.
I don't turn around to see her wrinkled face.
The smell of grease pulls me
out of my dream. I stay awake for a long time
until my feet grow warm.

V.

When the rice paper falls in the pool, water
presses hard against the fibers that connect its life.
When it dries, its shape appears again with uneven
skin and wrinkles and scars from the violence of the water.
All the bones joined tighter
without a space for softness, like our memories.
Nothing will undo our old loving.

Remembering Williams

'Wish we could talk today'
you wrote—no more
than that: the time before
it was: 'I stumbled
on a poem you had written', but the theme
lost itself, you forgot to say
what it was
'that called to mind
something over which
we had both been working, but had not
worked out by half.' Your wife
said she had done her mourning
while you still lived. Life
is a hard bed to lie on dying.

A Confession

for W.C.W.

I fell asleep, reading your new book.
It's
a gift, to be able to fall asleep almost
anywhere.
I was lying on a riverbank,
within the sound of a waterfall,
listening
to the water. And to your words.
The
recurrence of the phrases. The currency of
the thought.
It's one of life's greatest
pleasures, to be able to sleep of an
afternoon.
To read your poems. To hear your
voice.
To sleep, when tired. To wake,
refreshed.

Walking with Dr. Williams

He bids farewell
to the crying babies,
impetigo, scabies

ringworm, croup, hives,
the spider bites
gone haywire

bundles the Number 4 sutures
into antiseptic drawers,
locks the tetracycline,

penicillin behind glass doors,
stows the steel needles
in their steam autoclave

while upstairs Flossie prepares
the butcher block table:
salmon cakes, baby peas, pommes dauphine.

At dusk we roam
the banks of the Passaic
where a cojo fisherman

calls out some lines
from Longfellow:
Like a huge organ, rise the burnished arms . . .

He bows and smiling passes,
  says how like a kumquat
    the fisherman's bell

dangling from grocery cart.
  He dares me to shout
    the names of what we see

and I do:
  gaggle of geese, dusty miller, cumulonimbus . . .
    We dissect the day's words:

Viburnum, saxifrage, intracutaneous,
  our tongues larded
    with dactyls, trochees.

Late at night in the damp attic
  at a desk where Flossie has placed
    almond cookies and Twinings with real cream,

he will clip the Dow Jones Index,
  tape it to a wall,
    wrap a blanket around his shoulders, write

    The instant

trivial as it is

          is all we have

                unless, unless

Plums

Sweet plums of New Jersey the girls eat them at evening
they eat plums at midday and morning they eat plums at night
they suck and they bite
they draw the latch-string on the door of sense in the clouds
Doctor Williams lives in the house with his poems he washes his hands
he washes his hands when it's too dark to write
he steps into the yard past the wheelbarrow bits of broken green bottle glass shining
he whistles the branches to rain down the plums
he whistles the branches to rain down the babies
he tells them the babies are plums

Sweet plums of New Jersey we eat you at night
we eat you at morning and midday we eat you at evening
we suck bite and spit out the flesh-threaded stone
Doctor Williams lives in the house he washes his hands after delivering babies
he writes poems when it grows dark your fair-haired daughter
your dark-eyed son we shut the door to the news it is difficult to get from poems
he shouts branches shake furious girls hold out your aprons
he holds his palms open to the sky his hands are clean
trees rustle your heart-shaped leaves girls gather your children

Cold plums of New Jersey we eat you all night
all midday and morning and evening we eat
dust off the white bloom run our thumbs along clefts
Doctor Williams lives in the house your fair-haired daughter
your dark-eyed son he writes wheelbarrow songs
he shouts rock-a-bye boughs break Making is a woman in blue
bring her paper to sketch the plum blossoms shaking
erasing the sky we must fill with plums poems babies

Sweet plums of New Jersey all night until morning
we eat you the woman holds out her sky-colored skirts
we eat you at dusk and daybreak we gorge glut we slurp
and our Making is a woman in blue who holds out her skirts
she wipes clean the paper trees sky our sticky hands fills our aprons again
Doctor Williams lives in the house my fair-haired daughter
he looses the branches the stars the broken green bottle bits shine
he dandles babies stacks alphabet blocks says a fine one yes ma'am!
our Making is a woman in a sky-colored skirt
my fair-haired daughter
my dark-eyed son

The Nostalgias of Change

to William Carlos Williams

Now traffic rumbles past a wide front porch
at Rutherford to tunnel to New York
from Jersey flats, the sea-swamped earth, crisp weeds
around the junk-yards, gas-tanks, chemicals,
highways as tricky as Russian roulette . . .
All towns across this Country are alike:
Main Streets with shops thin out to mansions where
Victorian facades take tourists in.
Change, like a bombing, hollows neighborhoods
with car-parks. Change, eating out Tradition
like a rust scraped clean as steel, keeps moving,
bumper-to-bumper, just to see new sights.
The Tudor-Gothic home of 1905
corners the old where King and Queen Streets cross,
just as it should. The railroad line cuts round
the outskirts. Downtown, the sooty train-shred dusts
the demolition crew. As maudlin as
a heart-laced Valentine, a sentiment
involves the typical, not beautiful.
The recent past sheds gaslit living-rooms
of horsehair sofas, doilies, plum plush chairs,
grandmotherly, maternal, just as though
a poet put aside his stereopticon,
decided what was basic, and went on from there.

Old Sycamore

In memory of Joel Oppenheimer, 1930–88

The slender young
sycamores of Rutherford,
New Jersey, are fat

now, trunks
scarred, half dead,
no longer

there. The poems
Williams left

behind, always new
in themselves,

are old
too. What I fear
is that our
language,

possessed
of so much

light that it
has filled
the world with

things
we *must* be
told of,

now
battered by
decades of
persuasion,

can no longer
make a thing
so clear I am

overwhelmed by
its clarity, can

no longer make
a thing into
a word spoken

once and within
that single
utterance

repeated, over
and over, until
it reaches, then

exceeds its own
self-meaning
and we lose

sight
of it, begin
to see instead,
everything around

it—a whole
world of new

things made from
an old thing
brought into

being in one
single beat

of existence
—the offering,
then, of a

thing
left behind.

"Not in ideas . . ."

"Try medicine, why don't you! Lots to keep you busy, and lots to make you think."
—William C. Williams to Robert Coles, as quoted in Coles' *The Mind's Fate*

"But what do they mean . . . his poems . . .
I mean?" The young man in the second
row fixed his dark eyes on me just as
I was about to move from "Nantucket,"
and "The Red Wheelbarrow" to Roethke

and Bishop. Unconvinced that a poem
might just be images felt and stored, he
kept at it. Students stabbed and chewed,
tossing thoughts. The young man's
expression softened a bit. We moved on.

Yet here I am weeks later, watching March
wind sweep cherry blossoms like snow
across the yard, remembering the lavender
and yellow flowers, an immaculate white bed
and fresh curtains, thinking of a doctor's days

jammed with swabbing, prescribing, driving,
jotting, his exhaustion evaporating
as he entered that airy room, letting the open
window bathe him in things he would take in
and away—the key, tray, tumbler and glass,

before taking himself out into late afternoon light.
The rare moments between dying patients,
fragile newborns, when he slipped out
one Paterson door after another, seizing
images like a cane for balance on his way

from one house call to the next. A doctor
reminding himself as often as he did
others of essential things—a sparrow,
an iris, simplicity and generosity in
'our daily conduct,' snatching moments,

scratching notes between patients. Only now
watching drifting blossoms do I realize
that we did not linger long enough over
a young man's question or the busy doctor
who would have found the time to answer it.

Doctor Bill Williams

There was once upon a time a man who lost the
Dictionary and he kept saying ladies and gentlemen
I have nothing up my sleeves and the audience smiled
Since the children were present and after all the children
Were happy and the happiness of children is a serious matter
If one lives in Rutherford New Jersey and owns a car and
Can never be caught in the wrong church on Sunday I mean
That if you suddenly saw a field of sunflowers and
Remembered your wife telling the maid that your room
Must be cleaned this time as a room should be cleaned
And absolutely you cannot keep that appointment with
Mrs. MacFalley the woman with waved hair and slim
Everything besides the taxes are due on the
Thirty-first and the mirrors forget everything they see.

For William Carlos Williams

The last, absolutely the last
dahlia

on Ridge Road, Rutherford, New Jersey,
    October 18, 1960,

you have outlived it
and wear the epaulet
to prove it

I salute you in your
Garden State

You taught us to
scrape all the leaves off the bottom of the barrel
because the leaves can equal

the sacred red anemones of Osiris
falling in the blue waterfalls of
Lebanon

and you knew it

The Oldest Garden in the World

Something drives out
from the fate I was hungry for
A body that fulfills its face
carries into day
what fades behind it
In *Natural History*
Sophocles loved
Asphodel, but Asphodel
loved William Carlos
Williams as hyacinth
loved France, and honey
loves a toothache
Is that a crime
or just a form of currency
like big tobacco moving on
with shady radar
over our greenery?

Song

Now the precise, remote, and
striking coolness of
fine wood is in the air
sunrise is set as if
reflected from a
violin hung in the
trees—the birds are
lost in admiration in a
stiff wild hall of light

And I preach to them of
the mystery of this my
sacred craft but no one
listens
I a poet
stand about the streets
alive for any audience
and shivering at quiet
as at pure thin morning

W.C.W. Watching Presley's Second Appearance on *The Ed Sullivan Show*: Mercy Hospital, Newark, 1956

The tube,
like the sonnet,
is a fascist form.
I read they refused
to show the kid's
wiggling bum.
"The pure products
of American . . ."
etc.
From Mississippi!
Tupelo,
a name like a flower
you wouldn't want
beside you
in a room
like this,
where the smell holds you
a goddamn
hostage to yourself,
where talk's
no longer cheap.
Missed connections,
missed connections—
a junk heap
blazing there in
Ironbound,
a couple kids

beside it
juiced on the
cheapest wine. Mid-
thought. Midwinter,
and stalled
between the TV screen
and window . . .
The pomped-up kid,
who preens
and tells us
"Don't be cruel."
Kid, forget it.
you don't know
a fucking thing
about cruelty yet.

Homage to William Carlos Williams

I THE BODY

You removed integument.
You palpated red fibrils,
extracted breastplates,
exposed diaphragms.
You saw the once rhythmic heart
still silent, again and again, in a pool of formalin.

We begin the study of life
with our hands buried in the dead.
This is how you did it
and how we will always do it.
The body refuses the name *body*,
taking *cadaver*, meaning *to fall*.

II CORPUS

Nothing could keep you away.
Not *Histology*. Not *Gray's Anatomy*.
You filled the margins of *Physiology*

with notes for poems.
Nothing could keep you away.
Not surgery. Not psychiatry. Not pediatrics.

Not the blankness of corridors.
Not the doctors you called teacher.
Not the New Jersey days silenced by snow.

Nothing could keep you away.
Not the little girl bundled against the winter sunlight.
Not the yellow wheel barrow outside her window.

III THE BODY IN BLOOM

Geneva, the Lycée Condorcet in Paris,
the snow erasing everything. . .
how easily you forgot
the scholastic virtue of travelling.
You did not question the lizards

that ate contradictions
—both flies and flower buds—
the way *corpus* encompassed
not only art but the body
silent in the morgue.

You did not question
the truth of liver,
the truth of lungs,
the truth of blood when we are cut
so the body blooms.

Homage to William Carlos Williams

Where I park
the grass today
is lit with pink

magnolia petals
same as the black
Chevy Impala

dotted with green
bud husks from
a maple and

in clear puddles
on the black
asphalt the gray

spring sky is
strangely mirrored—
a song that gives

the world right
back to itself
or the endless

cries the killdeer
cry around us
here—cries

neither sad nor
happy, cries
violent and sweet

as spring itself
wild with
wanting to live.

A Letter to William Carlos Williams

We know, Doctor Williams, you and I
as we go
from patient one to next,
thumb
the rumpled charts, cough
nervously and look away from worried eyes,
what
we will see—

What is, is, and it is
just this: the
truth
of blood and flesh we wrestle with:
sheer, brute, singular,
wounded—

ourselves.

Bookmark, *Selected Poems*, William Carlos Williams

From dry fragile still
fragrant yellow-

green stalks & leaves placed
between *the descent*

of winter & the locust tree
in flower stems

the scent of spring.

Commercial Poem

William Carlos Williams, an old man
now, over one hundred years old,
is forced out of retirement and death
and endorses frozen food products
for companies catering to upwardly
mobile America, or so it seems after
I watched the late movie last night
and saw this ad for waffles that opened
with an old woman who was probably
Flossie reading a note she found
on the fridge outloud, saying
"this is just to say
I have eaten the waffles
that were in the freezer
and which you
were probably saving
for brunch: forgive me,
they were fluffy and
light, and very inexpensive" but
she could have been anybody, an actress
playing Flossie, not necessarily her.

Then he appeared, William Carlos Williams,
over one hundred years old and tired,
saying "this is one pure product
of America I go crazy for" and trying
to smile, pretending the earth under
our feet is the crust of some huge American
apple pie, and I groaned when I saw

him on TV and wished the commercial
would end, but the image lingered on
the screen, all night he was there, smiling
at Flossie with no life in his old
physician's eye, and an ache in his
gypsy heart.

Keats to Williams

In a letter to his friend Benjamin Bailey, November 22, 1817, John Keats writes about the Imagination. It's all he wants to speak of, he excitedly asserts. Then he suddenly exclaims, "O for a life of Sensations rather than of Thoughts!" We know the importance of Keats to the young William Carlos Williams, whose first book, *Poems* (1909), was (he wrote), "Bad Keats, nothing else—oh, well, bad Whitman too."

During his intern days in New York, Dr. Williams worked on a long poem inspired by Keats' *Endymion*, about a young prince saved from poisoning by his old nurse. The young man wanders through a strange world, vaguely remembering the catastrophe.

A few short years later, by 1917 and the book *Al Que Quiere!*, Williams has purified his style of archaisms, Keatsisms, and the troubadorisms of his friend Ezra Pound. Ten years later he insists: "Say it! No idea but in things." He demands it twice in the same poem, *Paterson*: "Say it! No ideas but in things."

Now here's my point: aren't the statements of these two poets essentially the same, the first translated out of Keats' romantic into Williams' demotic language? Keats might have addressed that letter to Williams, and in a sense, he did.

I lay these lines side by side by two poets that I love—the young man who never grew old, the old man who always stayed young:

"O for a life of Sensations rather than of Thoughts!"

"Say it! No ideas but in things."

Facing It

The young doctor is dancing with happiness
in the sparkling wind, alone
at the prow of the ferry.
—William Carlos Williams

W. 230 Street, a narrow lane on the ridge
at Spuyten Duyvil, and the view is east, a half mile out
to the next hill, a fortress of apartments, layers
of brick and glass, thick walls in shadow. It is dawn.
Quietly the city I will enter waits.

Broadway is in the valley at my feet,
and from here a step-street takes me down.
Behind thin glass and under quilts
children wait to enter the ten thousand classrooms.
The platform of the Broadway El is filling

and I'm reciting a poem myself, looking out
to the hills of Van Cortland Park. A train is not coming.
I know none of the people here, and they keep arriving.
This year I do know 150 children's names,
and their facts will emerge like riddles, like potholes,

like felonies, like fresh flowers, like new music
I will have to hear and hear and hear.
I am not young, and I am not dancing
on the El platform. I am waiting.
I will know the living music when it starts.

notes on contributors 

A. R. AMMONS (1926–2001) was born in North Carolina. After serving in World War II, he earned degrees in biology and English. In 1964 he began teaching at Cornell, from which he retired in 1998 as Goldwin Smith Professor of English and Poet in Residence. He is the author of more than twenty-five collections of poetry, including, most recently, *Selected Poems* (2006), edited by David Lehman.

RANE ARROYO (1954–2010) was born in Chicago and received his Ph.D. from the University of Pittsburgh. Arroyo won the Carl Sandburg Poetry Prize for his 1997 collection *The Singing Shark*, and the 2004 John Ciardi Poetry Prize for his collection *The Portable Famine*. He is the author of a collection of short stories, *How to Name a Hurricane* (2005), and his most recent collection of poems is *The Buried Sea: New and Selected Poems* (2009). At the time of his sudden death in May 2010, Arroyo was professor of English at the University of Toledo.

JOHN ASHBERY was born in Rochester, New York, and was educated at Harvard and Columbia. In the 1950s and 1960s he lived in France and worked as an art critic for the European edition of the *New York Herald Tribune*, returning to the United States to write art criticism for *New York*, *Newsweek*, and *ARTNews*. He has taught at Brooklyn College and Bard and served as poet laureate of New York from 2001 to 2003. In 1975 *Self-Portrait in a Convex Mirror* won the triple crown of poetry, receiving the Pulitzer Prize, the National Book Award, and the National Book Critics Circle Award. He is the author of more than thirty collections of poems, essays, and prose. The first volume of his *Collected Poems* was published in 2008. He lives in New York City and Hudson, New York.

TONY BARNSTONE was born in Middletown, Connecticut, and raised in Bloomington, Indiana. For years he lived in Greece, Spain, Kenya, and China before taking his M.A. in English and creative writing and Ph.D. in English literature at the University of California, Berkeley. He is the author of four full-length books of poems, the most recent of which is *Tongue of War* (2009), winner of the 2008 John Ciardi Prize in Poetry. His most recent books of translation include *Chinese Erotic Poems* (2007) and *The Anchor Book of Chinese Poetry* (2005). He is the Albert Upton Professor of English Language and Literature at Whittier College.

WILLIS BARNSTONE was born in Lewiston, Maine, and educated at Bowdoin, Columbia, and Yale. He taught in Greece at the end of the civil war (1949–1951), in Buenos Aires during the Dirty War, and in China during the Cultural Revolution, where he was later a Fulbright Professor of American Literature at Beijing Foreign Studies University (1984–1985). His publications include more than forty-five collections of poems, edited anthologies, scholarship, and translations, including, most recently, *Ancient Greek Lyrics* (2009), *Sweet Bitter Love: Poems of Sappho* (2004), *Sonnets to Orpheus: Rainer Maria Rilke* (2004), and *Border of a Dream: Selected Poems of Antonio Machado* (2004). His literary translations of the New Testament include *The Restored New Testament: A New Translation with Commentary, Including the Gnostic Gospels Thomas, Mary, and Judas* (2009) and *The New Covenant: The Four Gospels and Apocalypse* (2002).

DENNIS BARONE was born in Teaneck, New Jersey, and grew up in Teaneck and Ramsey. In high school he ran in the New Jersey cross-country finals in the park in Paterson. With James Finnegan he coedited *Visiting Wallace: Poems Inspired by the Life and Work of Wallace Stevens* (2009). He is the author of a collection of selected poems, *Parallel Lines* (2011), and *America/Trattabili* (2010), a study of Italian American narrative. He is director of American studies at Saint Joseph College in West Hartford, Connecticut.

JEFFERY BEAM is the author of over twenty works of poetry and musical collaborations including, most recently, *Gospel Earth* (2010), *MountSeaEden* (2010), and *An Invocation* (2009). His spoken-word CD with multimedia, *What We Have Lost: New & Selected Poems 1977–2001*, was a 2003 Audio Publishers Award finalist. He edited the book version of the 2010 *Jacket* magazine feature *The Lord of Orchards: Jonathan Williams at Eighty*, and *Blue Darter—Jonathan Williams: A Bibliography of the Publications & Ephemera, 1950–2008*. He is a botanical librarian in the Biology-Chemistry Library at the University of North Carolina–Chapel Hill.

MARVIN BELL's nineteenth book was the wartime collection *Mars Being Red*

(2007). His twentieth collection is a collaboration titled *7 Poets, 4 Days, 1 Book* (2009), coauthored with poets from Hungary, Malta, Russia, and Slovenia, as well as the United States. He has collaborated with photographers, musicians, composers, and dancers—most recently with the singer Marvin Tate and the composer David Gompper—and performs periodically with the bassist Glen Moore of the jazz group Oregon. Bell is the creator of a poetic form known as the "dead man poems." He taught for forty years for the University of Iowa Writer's Workshop. He lives with his wife, Dorothy, in Iowa City and Port Townsend, Washington.

CHARLES BERNSTEIN is author of *All the Whiskey in Heaven: Selected Poems* (2010), *Blind Witness: Three American Operas* (2008), *Girly Man* (2006), and *My Way: Speeches and Poems* (1999). He is Donald T. Regan Professor of English and Comparative Literature at the University of Pennsylvania.

TED BERRIGAN (1934–1983) was born in Providence, Rhode Island. After serving in the army during the Korean War, he returned to the United States and finished his B.A. and M.A. at the University of Tulsa. He is the author of more than twenty collections of poetry, including *The Sonnets* (1964) and *The Collected Poems of Ted Berrigan* (2005). Berrigan is often associated with the second generation of the New York School of Poets that included Ron Padgett, Anne Waldman, Jim Carroll, and Anselm Hollo.

ELEANOR BERRY lives and writes in rural Lyons, Oregon. She holds a Ph.D. in English, and much of her published scholarship has revolved around the free verse and prosody innovations of William Carlos Williams, George Oppen, Lorine Niedecker, and Charles Olson. Her collection of poems is titled *Green November* (2007).

WENDELL BERRY—poet, essayist, novelist, farmer—was born in Newcastle, Kentucky, and has lived on a farm in Port Royal, Kentucky, for more than forty years. He is the author of more than thirty books of poetry, most recently *Leavings: Poems* (2009); more than a dozen collections of short stories and novels, including *That Distant Land: The Collected Stories* (2005); and more than twenty-five collections of essays and prose, most recently, *Imagination in Place* (2010).

JOHN BERRYMAN (1914–1972) received the Pulitzer Prize for 77 *Dream Songs* in 1965. At the time of his death in 1972, the number of dream songs had grown to 385. Among his collections of poetry are *Homage to Mistress Bradstreet*

(1956); *Berryman's Sonnets* (1967); *The Dream Songs* (1969), winner of the National Book Award; and *His Toy, His Dream, His Rest* (1968). *John Berryman: Collected Poems 1937–1971*, edited by Charles Thornbury, was published in 1991. Berryman also is the author of a novel, *Recovery* (1973). Paul Mariani's biography, *Dream Song: The Life of John Berryman*, was published in 1996.

PAUL BLACKBURN (1926–1971) was born in St. Albans, Vermont. He graduated from the University of Wisconsin in 1950. After hitching several times to Washington, D.C., to visit Ezra Pound in St. Elizabeth's Hospital, Blackburn became acquainted with the work of Cid Corman, Robert Creeley, Charles Olson, Denise Levertov, Joel Oppenheimer, and Jonathan Williams, and later became involved with them. He was also a noted translator (*Poem of the Cid*, Federico García Lorca, Octavio Paz, Julio Cortázar, Pablo Picasso). *The Collected Poems of Paul Blackburn* was published in 1984. His son, Carlos Blackburn, was named after William Carlos Williams.

ROBERT BLY's most recent books include *Reaching Out to the World: New and Selected Prose Poems* (2009) and *The Angels Knocking on the Tavern Door: Thirty Poems of Hafez*, translated with Leonard Lewisohn (2009). With Anne Wright, he edited *Selected Poems by James Wright* (2005). In 2008 Bly was named Minnesota's first poet laureate.

KAY BOYLE (1902–1992) was born in Minneapolis, Minnesota, and grew up in Cincinnati, Ohio. A prolific writer, she is the author of more than fifty books, including novels, novellas, short stories, memoirs, books for children, essays, and poetry. After World War II, she was a European correspondent for the *New Yorker*, and later was blacklisted during the McCarthy era. A political activist during the 1960s, Boyle taught for many years at San Francisco State (College) University. Sandra Whipple Spanier's *Kay Boyle, Artist and Activist* (1986) is an excellent biography. *Collected Poems of Kay Boyle* was published in 1991.

RICHARD BRAUTIGAN (1935–1984) was born in Tacoma, Washington, and grew up in Washington and Oregon, eventually settling in San Francisco in the mid-1950s. During his short life, he wrote ten novels, ten collections of poetry, a collection of short stories, and several collections of nonfiction. He achieved international recognition and eventually cultlike status with the publication of *Trout Fishing in America* (1967). Among his collections of poems are *The Pill versus the Springhill Mine Disaster* (1968), *Rommel Drives on Deep into Egypt*

(1970), and *Loading Mercury with a Pitchfork* (1976). He can be heard on the recording *Listening to Richard Brautigan* (record album, 1970; CD, 2005).

MICHAEL J. BUGEJA is director of the Greenlee School of Journalism and Communication at Iowa State University. He is the author of twenty books, many of them in the field of technology and communications, including the acclaimed *Interpersonal Divide: The Search for Community in a Technological Age* (2005). He is the author of *The Art and Craft of Poetry* (2001) and *Poet's Guide: How to Publish and Perform Your Work* (1995). His collections of poems include *The Visionary* (1995) and *Millennium's End: Poems* (1999).

JOHN CIARDI (1916–1986) was born in Boston, the son of Italian immigrants. He earned degrees from Tufts University and the University of Michigan. During World War II, he was a B-29 gunner, flying more than twenty missions over Japan. Several generations of poetry students were raised on his classic textbook, *How Does a Poem Mean?* (1960; repr., 1975). Known as one of the finest translators of Dante's *The Divine Comedy*, Ciardi also published more than twenty-five collections of poems and more than a dozen collections of poems for children, and edited or coauthored more than twenty collections of essays and anthologies. *The Collected Poems of John Ciardi* was published in 1997.

CID CORMAN (1924–2004) was born in Boston and studied at Tufts University and the University of Michigan. A highly influential editor and publisher, Corman, in 1951, started the magazine *Origin* (and later Origin Press), which published the work of Paul Blackburn, Robert Creeley, Robert Duncan, Denise Levertov, Lorine Niedecker, Charles Olson, Gary Snyder, Wallace Stevens, and William Carlos Williams, and many other writers associated with the Beats, Objectivists, and the Black Mountain Poets. His many collections of poems and translations from the French and Japanese include *The Next One Thousand Years: The Selected Poems of Cid Corman* (2008), *OF* (2 vols., 1990), *Backroads to Far Towns: Basho's Travel Journal* (1996), *Things: Selected Writings of Francis Ponge* (1986), *Asking Myself, Answering Myself* by Shinpei Kusano (1984), *Livingdying* (1970), and *Sun Rock Man* (1962). He lived and worked in Kyoto for nearly three decades.

ROBERT CREELEY (1926–2005) was born in Arlington, Massachusetts. After attending Harvard and working for the American Field Service in Burma and India in the late 1940s, he eventually earned his B.A. from Black Mountain

College, where he later taught and was associated with the Black Mountain School of writers and artists. In 1949 he began corresponding with William Carlos Williams. Williams told Robert Creeley, "You have the subtlest feeling for the measure I have encountered anywhere except in the verses of Ezra Pound." Creeley's lifelong friendship with the poet and teacher Charles Olson is reflected in the multivolume *Charles Olson and Robert Creeley: The Complete Correspondence* (1996). He published more than sixty books of poetry, including *A Form of Women* (1959), *For Love: Poems 1950–1960* (1962), *Selected Poems* (1976), and *The Collected Poems of Robert Creeley, 1945–1975* (1982).

BARBARA CROOKER's collections include *More* (2010), *Line Dance* (2008), and *Radiance* (2005). Her poems have appeared in numerous anthologies, magazines, and chapbooks and have been featured on Garrison Keillor's *The Writer's Almanac*. She lives in Fogelsville, Pennsylvania.

TODD DAVIS was born in Elkhart County, Indiana. He is the author of three books of poetry, including *The Least of These* (2009) and *Some Heaven* (2007). Most recently, he coedited *Making Poems—40 Poems with Commentary by the Poets* (2010). In addition to his creative work, Davis is the author or editor of six scholarly books. He teaches creative writing, environmental studies, and American literature at Penn State University's Altoona College.

GREG DELANTY was born in Cork, Ireland, in 1958 and lives in Burlington, Vermont, where he teaches at Saint Michael's College. He became an American citizen in 1994. His latest books are *Collected Poems 1986–2006* (2006), *The Selected Poems of Kyriakos Charalambides in Translation* (2005), and *The Ship of Birth* (2003; repr., 2007).

THOMAS DISCH (1940–2008) was born in Des Moines, Iowa, and later moved with his family to Minneapolis, Minnesota. He was a prolific writer, known for his science fiction writing as well as his poetry, publishing more than twenty novels and novellas, a dozen collections of poetry, seven short story collections, four books for children, four collections of essays, and two plays. He was a regular book and theater reviewer for the *Nation*, *Harper's*, the *Washington Post*, the *Los Angeles Times*, the *New York Times*, the *Times Literary Supplement*, and *Entertainment Weekly*. *Winter Journey*, a collection of thirty-one poems by Disch, with photographs and film by Eric Solstein, was published in 2009.

NORMAN DUBIE was born in Barre, Vermont. Among his many collections of poems are *The Mercy Seat: Collected & New Poems 1967–2001* (2001) and *The*

Insomniac Liar of Topo (2007). He is Regents' Professor of English at Arizona State University.

STEPHEN DUNN was born in Forest Hills, New York, and earned his B.A. in history from Hofstra University in 1962. He attended the New School from 1964 to 1966 and received his M.A. in creative writing from Syracuse University in 1970. He is the author of sixteen books, including *Different Hours* (2000), which won the 2001 Pulitzer Prize for poetry. Since 1974 he has taught at Richard Stockton College of New Jersey, where he is Distinguished Professor of Creative Writing. He also has been a visiting professor at the University of Washington, New York University, Columbia, and the University of Michigan. *What Goes On: Selected & New Poems 1995–2009* (2009) was chosen as one of two Notable Books of the Year in Poetry by the American Library Association. His most recent collection of poems is *Here and Now* (2011).

RICHARD EBERHART (1904–2005) was born in Austin, Minnesota, and graduated from Dartmouth College. His long and distinguished career began with the publication of his first book of poetry, *A Bravery of Earth* (1930). He succeeded Robert Frost as poetry consultant to the Library of Congress from 1959 to 1961. His *Selected Poems, 1930–1965* (1965) won the Pulitzer Prize for poetry in 1966, and his *Collected Poems, 1930–1976* (1976) received the National Book Award in 1977. He served as New Hampshire's poet laureate from 1979 to 1984 and was elected to the American Academy of Arts and Letters in 1982. *New and Selected Poems: 1930–1990* was published in 1990.

HEID E. ERDRICH, a member of the Turtle Mountain Band of Ojibway, grew up in Wahpeton, North Dakota. She earned degrees from Dartmouth College and the Johns Hopkins University Writing Seminars. She is the author of three poetry collections: *National Monuments* (2009), *The Mother's Tongue* (2005), and *Fishing for Myth* (1997; repr., 2010). She also coedited *Sister Nations: Native American Women on Community* (2002). With her sister Louise Erdrich, she is the cofounder and owner of Birchbark Books in Minneapolis, Minnesota, and Birchbark House, a nonprofit clearinghouse for indigenous language–centered literature.

SUSAN FIRER is the recipient of the 2008 Lorine Niedecker Poetry Award. She is the author of *Milwaukee Does Strange Things to People: New & Selected Poems 1979–2007* (2007), *The Laugh We Make When We Fall* (2002), and *The Lives of the Saints and Everything* (1993). "Call Me Pier," published here, is included in the Poetry Everywhere series, available for viewing on YouTube or through the Poetry Foundation. She teaches at the University of Wisconsin–Milwaukee. She was poet laureate of the city of Milwaukee from 2008 to 2010.

ANN FISHER-WIRTH's third book of poems is *Carta Marina* (2009). She is the author of the book-length study *William Carlos Williams and Autobiography: The Woods of His Own Nature* (1989), and has written many scholarly articles on Williams as well. A former Fulbright scholar to Switzerland and Sweden, she teaches at the University of Mississippi.

ALICE FRIMAN was born and raised in New York City. She earned a B.A. from Brooklyn College and an M.A. from Butler University in Indianapolis, Indiana. From 1971 to 1993 she taught at the University of Indianapolis. She is the author of eight collections of poetry, most recently *Vinculum* (2011), *The Book of the Rotten Daughter* (2006), and *Zoo* (1999), winner of the Ezra Pound Poetry Award from Truman State University, and the Sheila Margaret Motton Prize from the New England Poetry Club. Professor emerita at the University of Indianapolis, she now lives in Milledgeville, Georgia, where she is poet-in-residence at Georgia College & State University.

ROBERT GIBB was born in the steel town of Homestead, Pennsylvania. He is the author of seven books of poetry, among them *What the Heart Can Bear: Selected and Uncollected Poems 1979–1993* (2009) and *The Origins of Evening* (1998), a National Poetry Series Winner. He lives on New Homestead Hill above the Monongahela River.

ALLEN GINSBERG (1926–1997) was born in Newark, New Jersey. After graduating from Paterson's East Side High School in 1943, Ginsberg attended Columbia College in New York, where he met William S. Burroughs, Neal Cassady, and Jack Kerouac. On March 28, 1950, a twenty-three-year-old Ginsberg heard William Carlos Williams speak at the Guggenheim Museum. Too shy to introduce himself to Williams, Ginsberg wrote a letter of introduction two days later, beginning a mentorship that would last until Williams's death in 1963. Ginsberg claimed that Williams helped him to free his voice, allowing him to write in the style that made Ginsberg famous in his debut collection, *Howl and Other Poems* (1956), for which Williams wrote the foreword, remarking, "Hold back the edges of your gowns, Ladies, we are going through hell." Williams also wrote the introduction to Ginsberg's *Empty Mirror* (1961). Williams included some of Ginsberg's letters (including the one Ginsberg wrote on March, 30, 1950) in his epic poem *Paterson*. Among Ginsberg's numerous collections of poetry are *Kaddish and Other Poems* (1961); *Reality Sandwiches* (1963); *The Fall of America: Poems of These States, 1965–1971* (1973), winner of the National Book Award; and *Mind Breaths: Poems 1971–1976* (1976). *Collected Poems 1947–1997* was published in 2006. With Ann Waldman, he cofounded and directed the Jack Kerouac School of Disembodied Poetics at the Naropa University in Colorado, and later he became a Distinguished Professor at Brooklyn College.

PETER GIZZI was born and raised in Pittsfield, Massachusetts. He holds degrees from New York University, Brown University, and the State University of New York at Buffalo. His books include *The Outernationale* (2007), *Some Values of Landscape and Weather* (2003), *Artificial Heart* (1998), and *Periplum* (1992). He is also the editor of *The House That Jack Built: The Collected Lectures of Jack Spicer* (1998) and coeditor with Kevin Killian of *My Vocabulary Did This to Me: The Collected Poems of Jack Spicer* (2008). In 1994 he received the prestigious Lavan Younger Poet Award from the Academy of American Poets. He currently teaches at the University of Massachusetts, Amherst.

SUSAN GLICKMAN is the author of five collections of poems, including *Running in Prospect Cemetery: New and Selected Poems* (2004). A collection of her stories, *The Violin Lover* (2006), was the recipient of the Canadian Jewish Fiction Award. *The Picturesque & the Sublime: A Poetics of the Canadian Landscape* (1998) received the Gabrielle Prize for literary criticism and the Raymond Klibansky Prize for the humanities. She is also the author of a children's book, *Bernadette and the Lunch Bunch* (2008). She teaches writing at Ryerson University in Toronto, where she also works as a freelance editor. She is a former student of Denise Levertov, from whom she learned to love William Carlos Williams.

DAVID GRAHAM is the author of several books of poems, most recently *Stutter Monk* (2000), and an essay anthology coedited with Kate Sontag, *After Confession: Poetry as Autobiography* (2001). He is professor of English at Ripon College in Ripon, Wisconsin, where he maintains an online poetry library that collects a wide variety of resources on poetry: http://web.mac.com/drjazz/iWeb/Site/DGPoLibrary.html.

MICHAEL HEFFERNAN was born and raised in Detroit, Michigan. He studied at the University of Detroit (A.B.) and the University of Massachusetts (Ph.D.), where he completed his doctorate with a dissertation on William Carlos Williams. Among his eight books are *The Cry of Oliver Hardy* (1979), *To the Wreakers of Havoc* (1984), *The Man at Home* (1988), *Love's Answer* (Iowa Poetry Prize, 1994), *The Night Breeze Off the Ocean* (2005), and his newest collection, *The Odor of Sanctity* (2008).

WILLIAM HEYEN lives in Brockport, New York. A former Senior Fulbright Lecturer in American literature in Germany, he is the editor of *September 11, 2001: American Writers Respond* (2002). Among his many collections of poetry are *The Confessions of Doc Williams & Other Poems* (2006); *Shoah Train* (2003), a finalist for the 2004 National Book Award; and *Erika: Poems of the Holocaust* (1984). In 2000 he retired from SUNY Brockport after thirty years of teaching creative writing and American literature.

EDWARD HIRSCH's most recent book is *The Living Fire: New and Selected Poems* (2010). He lives in New York and serves as president of the John Simon Guggenheim Memorial Foundation.

DANIEL HOFFMAN was born and educated in New York City, earning three degress from Columbia University. His first collection of poems, *An Armada of Thirty Whales* (1954), was chosen by W. H. Auden for the Yale Series of Younger Poets. Among his twelve collections of poems are *The Whole Nine Yards: Longer Poems* (2009), *Beyond Silence: Selected Shorter Poems, 1948–2003* (2003), and *Hang-Gliding from Helicon: New and Selected Poems* (1998). *Brotherly Love* (2000) was a finalist for both the National Book Award and the National Book Critics Circle Award. The best known of his six critical studies is *Poe Poe Poe Poe Poe Poe Poe* (1990), also a National Book Award finalist. Hoffman taught for ten years at Swarthmore College and then for twenty-seven years at the University of Pennsylvania, where he is Poet in Residence and Felix E. Schelling Professor of English Emeritus. He lives in Swarthmore, Pennsylvania, and on Cape Rosier in Maine.

DAVID IGNATOW (1914–1997) was born in Brooklyn, New York, and spent most of his life in the New York City area. William Carlos Williams reviewed Ignatow's first book, *Poems* (1948), for the *New York Times*, and the two became friends. He is the author of more than twenty collections of poems, including *Living Is What I Wanted: Last Poems* (1999), *At My Ease: Uncollected Poems of the Fifties and Sixties* (1998), *Against the Evidence: Selected Poems, 1934–1994* (1994), and *New and Collected Poems, 1970–1985* (1986). For many years he served as poetry editor for the *Nation*. He once wrote, "The modern poet most influential in my work was William Carlos Williams." In 1963, shortly after Williams's death, Ignatow edited *William Carlos Williams: A Memorial Chapbook*.

RODNEY JONES, born in rural Falkville, Alabama, was educated at the University of Alabama at Tuscaloosa and the University of North Carolina at Greensboro. He is the author of eight books of poetry: *Salvation Blues: 100 Poems, 1985–2005* (2006); *Kingdom of the Instant: Poems* (2004); *Elegy for the Southern Drawl* (1999), a finalist for the 2000 Pulitzer Prize; *Things That Happen Once* (1996); *Apocalyptic Narrative* (1993); *Transparent Gestures* (1989), winner of the 1989 National Book Critics Circle Award; *The Unborn* (1985); and *The Story They Told Us of Light* (1980). He teaches at Southern Illinois University.

JACK KEROUAC (1922–1969) is the author of more than thirty novels, collections of nonfiction, and poetry, including *On the Road* (1957) and *Mexico City Blues* (1959), which included three "choruses" for Williams, one of which is published here. In early 1957 Kerouac—along with Allen Ginsberg, Peter Orlovsky, and Gregory Corso—visited Williams and his wife at their home on 9 Ridge Road in Rutherford, New Jersey. Ginsberg would recall this visit later in "To WCW" (1970) and in the epigraph to the poem "Death News," included here.

GALWAY KINNELL, a former MacArthur Fellow and State Poet of Vermont, is the author of fourteen collections of poetry, including *Selected Poems* (1982), winner of the Pulitzer Prize and National Book Award in 1982. His most recent collection is *Strong Is Your Hold* (2006). He served as a chancellor of the Academy of American Poets from 2001 to 2007. He lives in New York City and Vermont.

KENNETH KOCH (1925–2002) is the author of many collections of poetry, including the epic *Ko, or A Season on Earth* (1959); *The Art of Love* (1975); and *New Addresses* (2000), a finalist for the National Book Award. *One Train* (1994) and *On the Great Atlantic Rainway: Selected Poems 1950–1988* (1994) earned him the Bollingen Prize in 1995, forty-two years after William Carlos Williams received it. *The Collected Poems of Kenneth Koch* (2005) and *On the Edge: Collected Long Poems* (2009) were published posthumously, and *The Collected Fiction of Kenneth Koch* was published in 2005. His books on teaching poetry and poetry writing to children and adults remain classics in the field:

Wishes, Lies, and Dreams (1970), *Rose, Where Did Your Get That Red?* (1973), *I Never Told Anybody* (1977), *Sleeping on the Wing* (1982), and *Making Your Own Days: The Pleasures of Reading and Writing Poetry* (1999).

KAREN KOVACIK directs the creative writing program at Indiana University–Purdue University Indianapolis. She is the author of two collections of poems, *Metropolis Burning* (2005) and *Beyond the Velvet Curtain* (1999). In 2004–2005 she held a Fulbright Research Grant to Warsaw, Poland, to translate contemporary Polish poetry, and her translations have appeared widely in the United States, the United Kingdom, and Italy.

MAXINE KUMIN was born in Germantown, Philadelphia. She earned her B.A. and M.A. from Radcliffe before it was subsumed by Harvard, and was a scholar in 1962–1963 at the Radcliffe Institute for Independent Study. Among her sixteen collections of poetry are *Where I Live: New and Select Poems 1990–2010* (2010), *Still to Mow* (2007), *Jack and Other New Poems* (2005), *Selected Poems 1960–1990* (1991), and *Up Country: Poems of New England* (1972), which was awarded the Pulitzer Prize in 1972. She also is the author of a memoir, *Inside the Halo and Beyond: Anatomy of a Recovery* (2000), about a nearly fatal carriage-driving accident, and the collections of essays, *Always Beginning: Essays on a Life in Poetry* (2000) and *Women, Animals, & Vegetables* (1996). In 1981–1982 she served as poet laureate of the United States. She and her husband live on a farm in Warner, New Hampshire.

JAMES LAUGHLIN (1914–1997) was born near Pittsburgh and began New Directions publishing company in 1936, when he was a student at Harvard, after studying with Ezra Pound and working for Gertrude Stein as her press agent and chauffeur. Laughlin's New Directions was founded to be a place where experimental writers could experiment. Among the many foreign writers who found their first American publisher in New Directions are Borges, Camus, Lorca, Mishima, Montale, Nabakov, Neruda, Pasternak, Paz, Rimbaud, and Sartre. For the most part, Laughlin was responsible for bringing William Carlos Williams's poetry, fiction, and essays into print. Their long and close friendship is the subject of Laughlin's memoir *Remembering William Carlos Williams* (1995), excerpted from his longer memoir, *By Ways* (2005). Laughlin is the author of eleven collections of poetry, including *Poems New and Selected* (1998) and *Love Poems* (1997), and three collections of prose, *Pound as Wuz* (1987), *Random Essays* (1989), and *Random Stories* (1990). Laughlin's selected letters to and from Williams, Kenneth Rexroth, Delmore Schwartz, Ezra Pound, Henry Miller, and Thomas Merton have been published in individual volumes.

DAVID LEHMAN is the series editor of *The Best American Poetry*, which he launched in 1988. Among his own collections of poetry are *Yeshiva Boys: Poems* (2009), *When a Woman Loves a Man* (2005), *The Evening Sun* (2002), and *The Daily Mirror: A Journal of Poetry* (2000). He is also the editor of *Great American Prose Poems: From Poe to the Present* (2003). *The Last Avant-Garde: The Making of the New York School of Poets* (1999) was named a "Book to Remember 1999" by the New York Public Library and remains the definitive study of those writers and that time. He teaches in the graduate writing programs at Bennington College and New School University. He lives in New York City.

GARY LEISING teaches at Utica College in New York. His poems have appeared in numerous magazines and journals, including *Barn Owl Review*, *Connecticut Review*, *Cincinnati Review*, *Quarterly West*, and *South Dakota Review*. His poems were chosen by Russell Edson for the 2008 1/2K Prize from *Indiana Review*.

DENISE LEVERTOV (1923–1997) was born in Ilford, Essex, United Kingdom, and moved to the United States in 1947, eventually becoming a naturalized American citizen in 1955. Among her many collections of poems are *With Eyes at the Back of Our Heads* (1959), *The Jacob's Ladder* (1961), *O Taste and See: New Poems* (1964), *To Stay Alive* (1971), *Collected Earlier Poems 1940–1960* (1979), *Candles in Babylon* (1982), and *This Great Unknowing: Last Poems* (2000). Her collections of essays include *The Poet in the World* (1973), *Light Up the Cave* (1981), and *New & Selected Essays* (1992). In 1998 Christopher MacGowan edited and wrote the introduction to *The Letters of Denise Levertov and William Carlos Williams*.

PHILIP LEVINE is the author of seventeen collections of poetry, most recently *News of the World* (2009). He is a two-time recipient of the National Book Award: *Ashes* (1980) and *What Work Is* (1991). *The Simple Truth* (1995) was the recipient of the Pulitzer Prize. He divides his time between Fresno, California, and Brooklyn, New York.

LYN LIFSHIN was born in Barre, Vermont. She is the author of more than 125 collections of poems, among them *Another Woman Who Looks Like Me* (2006), *Before It's Light* (1999), *Cold Comfort: Selected Poems: 1970–1996* (1997), and, most recently, *Barbaro: Beyond Brokenness* (2009) and *The Licorice Daughter: My Year with Ruffian* (2005). An award-winning documentary of her life, *Lyn Lifshin: Not Made of Glass*, was released in 1989. She lives in Virginia.

ROBERT LOWELL (1917–1977) was born in Boston. One of the most influential poets of the last half of the twentieth century, Lowell published many collections of poetry, prose, plays, and translations, including *Lord Weary's Castle* (1946), recipient of the Pulitzer Prize; *Life Studies* (1959), recipient of the National Book Award; *For the Union Dead* (1964); and *The Dolphin* (1973), also the recipient of the Pulitzer Prize. *Robert Lowell: Collected Poems*, edited by Frank Bidart and David Gewanter, was published in 2003.

LEZA LOWITZ is the author of *Yoga Poems: Lines to Unfold By* (2006) and *Green Tea to Go: Short Stories from Tokyo* (2004). She is the editor of *The Japan Journals 1947–2004*, by Donald Ritchie (2005), and the anthologies of contemporary Japanese women's poetry, *A Long Rainy Season* (1998) and *Other Side River* (1995). She lives in Tokyo, where she owns Sun and Moon Yoga Studio and continues to edit, translate, and interpret Japanese culture.

CLARENCE MAJOR—poet, painter, novelist, essayist, memoirist, anthologist—was born in Atlanta and raised in Chicago. He is the author of ten books of poetry, including *Myself Painting* (2008); *Configurations: New and Selected Poems, 1958–1998* (1998), a National Book Award Bronze Medal finalist; and *Waiting for Sweet Betty* (2002). He is also the author of critically acclaimed nonfiction and fiction and is editor of several landmark anthologies, including *The Garden Thrives: Twentieth-Century African-American Poetry* (1996), *Calling the Wind: Twentieth Century African-American Short Stories* (1993), and *Juba to Jive: Dictionary of Afro-American Slang* (1994). He is professor emeritus at the University of California, Davis. When he was starting out as a poet, Major corresponded with William Carlos Williams, who encouraged him.

PAUL MARIANI was born in New York City and grew up there and on Long Island. He is the author of six poetry collections, including *Deaths & Transfigurations* (2005), *The Great Wheel* (1996), and *Salvage Operations: New & Selected Poems* (1990). In addition to his monumental biography, *William Carlos Williams: A New World Naked* (1981; repr. 1990), which won the New Jersey Writers Award, was short-listed for an American Book Award, and was also named a *New York Times* Notable Book of the year, he is also the author of four other biographies: *Gerard Manley Hopkins: A Life* (2008); *The Broken*

Tower: A Life of Hart Crane (1999), a *New York Times* Notable Book of the year; *Lost Puritan: A Life of Robert Lowell* (1994), a *New York Times* Notable Book of the year; and *Dream Song: The Life of John Berryman* (1990). In 2009 he received the John Ciardi Award for Lifetime Achievement in Poetry. He was Distinguished University Professor at the University of Massachusetts, Amherst, where he taught from 1968 until 2000, and currently holds a chair in poetry at Boston College.

JOSEPH MASSEY was born in Chester, Pennsylvania, and lives in Humboldt, California. He is the author of a full-length collection of poems, *Areas of Fog* (2009), and many chapbooks and fine press editions, the latest of which is *The Lack Of* (2009).

PANSY MAURER-ALVAREZ was born in Puerto Rico and grew up in Lancaster, Pennsylvania. Her collections of poems include *Dolores: The Alpine Years* (1996) and *When the Body Says It's Leaving* (2004). She holds a B.A. from Carnegie Mellon University and has studied literature and languages in universities in Spain and Switzerland, where she worked as a teacher and translator before turning to writing full time in Paris, where she lives with her husband.

JAMES MERRILL (1926–1995)—recipient of the Bollingen Prize for Literature (1973), the Pulitzer Prize (1977), two National Book Awards (1967, 1979), and the National Book Critics Circle Award (1983)—was the author of more than thirty collections of poetry, plays, novels, and nonfiction. *Collected Poems* (2001), *Collected Novels and Plays* (2002), and *Collected Prose* (2004) were all edited by J. D. McClatchy and Stephen Yenser.

JOE MILUTIS is a media artist and writer whose interdisciplinary work includes experimental sound and radio; video works, for which he does his own music and sound design; new media; experimental narrative; theoretical writings; and various media and literature hybrids. *New Jersey as an Impossible Object* is an ongoing multimedia project, which uses William Carlos Williams's *Paterson* as a psychogeographical map for the city Paterson. His blog http://impossibleobject.blogspot.com/ documents the resonant space between the poem and its restless referent with audio, video, photos, and commentary. The project will culminate in a large-scale audio piece. He teaches audio art production, experimental media, and film studies classes at the University of South Carolina.

HILDA MORLEY (1916–1998) was born in New York City. She was educated in

Palestine, London, and Wellesley College. As a young child, she showed talent for poetry and corresponded with William Butler Yeats and H.D. Widely traveled, Morley worked as a translator and teacher, at one point teaching at Black Mountain College in the early 1950s. Her poetry fell under the poetic radar until the mid-1970s, when *A Blessing Outside Us* (1976), her first book of poetry, was published when she was sixty years old. Morley was married to the composer Stefan Wolpe, and many of her poems in her early books are about their life together and his illness and subsequent death. In an article she wrote about her own work, Morley said, "By my mid-thirties I was committed to a line derived from William Carlos Williams, making the rhythm of the poem out of the elements of ordinary speech." Morley's work was championed by Denise Levertov, who wrote a preface to her second collection, *What Are Winds and What Are Waters* (1983). *To Hold in My Hand: Selected Poems 1955–83*, with a preface by Stanley Kunitz, was published in 1984.

JOYCE CAROL OATES is an acclaimed novelist, essayist, poet, dramatist, and reviewer. She is the Roger S. Berlind Distinguished Professor of the Humanities at Princeton University and was the 2007 Humanist of the Year. Her most recent collection of poems is *Tenderness* (1996), and her most recent novel is *A Fair Maiden* (2010).

FRANK O'HARA (1926–1966) was born in Baltimore and grew up in Grafton, Massachusetts. He studied piano at the New England Conservatory in Boston. After serving in World War II in the South Pacific and Japan on the *USS Nicholas*, he matriculated to Harvard. In 1951 he earned an M.A. in English at the University of Michigan, and shortly thereafter moved to New York City, where he lived and worked until his death in 1966 at the age of forty. He was a reviewer for *ARTNews*, and in 1960 was assistant curator of painting and sculpture exhibitions for the Museum of Modern Art. While he was alive, he published several collections of poems, including *A City Winter and Other Poems* (1952), *Oranges: 12 Pastorals* (1953), *Meditations in an Emergency* (1957), *Second Avenue* (1960), and *Lunch Poems* (1964). Among his posthumous collections are *The Collected Poems of Frank O'Hara* (1971; repr., 1995), *The Selected Poems of Frank O'Hara* (1974), *Selected Plays* (1978), *Early Writing* (1977), *Amorous Nightmares of Delay: Selected Plays* (1997), and *Selected Poems* (2008). With John Ashbery, Barbara Guest, Kenneth Koch, and James Schuyler, O'Hara shared friendships and an aesthetic style and attitude that later would come to be known as the New York School of Poets. *City Poet: The Life and Times of Frank O'Hara*, a biography by Brad Gooch, was published in 1994.

CHARLES OLSON (1910–1970) was born in Worcester, Massachusetts. Educated at Wesleyan and Harvard, Olson went to work for the Foreign Language Division of the Office of War Information, eventually rising to assistant chief of the division. In 1944 he went to work for the Foreign Languages Division of the Democratic National Committee. By the late 1940s, dismayed with politics, Olson turned to full-time writing and teaching. His "Projective Verse" is one of the most influential essays of the last half of the twentieth century, shaping subsequent generations of poets. Among his many books are *The Maximus Poems* (1985), *The Collected Poems of Charles Olson, Excluding the Maximus Poems* (1987), *Collected Prose* (1997), and *Selected Letters* (2001). *Polis Is This: Charles Olson and the Persistence of Place*, a film about Olson directed by Henry Ferrini, was released in 2007.

JOEL OPPENHEIMER (1930–1988) was born and raised in Yonkers, New York. He was educated at Cornell University, the University of Chicago, and Black Mountain College in North Carolina, where he was a student of Charles Olson's. He was the first director of the Poetry Project at St. Mark's-in-the-Bowery Episcopal Church in Manhattan from 1966 to 1972, and from 1969 to 1984 he was a columnist for the *Village Voice*. Among his collections of poems are *The Women Poems* (1975), *Names & Local Habitations: Selected Earlier Poems 1951–1972* (1988), and *Collected Later Poems* (1997). He also was the author of two nonfiction collections, *Marilyn Lives*, about Marilyn Monroe (1981), and *The Wrong Season*, about the New York Mets' 1972 season (1973). A biography, *Don't Touch the Poet: The Life and Times of Joel Oppenheimer*, by Lyman Gilmore, was published in 1998.

LOUIS PHILLIPS is a poet, playwright, and short story writer whose most recent books are *The Woman Who Wrote King Lear and Other Stories* (2008); *The Kilroy Sonata*, a sequence of poems (2009); and *Fireworks in Some Particulars* (2009). He teaches at the School of Visual Arts in Manhattan.

EZRA POUND (1885–1972) was seventeen years old when he first met Williams, nineteen years old, at the University of Pennsylvania, and their literary friendship lasted for more than six decades. Pound was born in Hailey, Idaho. He moved with his family to a suburb of Philadelphia in 1889, earned a degree from Hamilton College in 1905, and moved to Venice, Italy, in 1908, eventually settling in London, where he began his program to change forever the course of modern poetry and literature. Among his more than sixty collections of poetry, criticism, and essays is *The Cantos*, Pound's 800+ page epic poem, published in its entirety (Cantos 1–117) in 1970. *Ezra Pound: Poems and Translations*, the most comprehensive collection of Pound's poems and translations (excluding *The Cantos*), was published in 2003.

TONY QUAGLIANO (1941–2007) is the author of four books of poetry, *Language Drawn and Quartered* (1975), *Fierce Meadows* (1981), *Snail Mail Poems* (1998), and *pictographs* (2008). He edited the special Bukowski issue of *Small Press Review*, which appeared in 1973. He edited *KAIMANA–The Journal of the Hawai'i Literary Arts Council* from 1990 to 2007, and was a contributing editor to the *Pushcart Prize: Best of the Small Presses* for thirty-three years.

F. D. REEVE worked on the docks for a short while before taking up an academic career. His is the author of three dozen books of poetry, fiction, criticism, and translation. After teaching in Columbia's Slavic department and Wesleyan's Russian department, he became a professor of letters at Wesleyan, from which he retired after a total of fifty years of academic service. His most recent collection of poems is *The Puzzle Master and Other Poems* (2010). His account of serving as Robert Frost's translator during Frost's 1962 trip to Russia at the invitation of President Kennedy, *Robert Frost in Russia* (1964), was reprinted with an introduction and notes in 2001.

KENNETH REXROTH (1905–1982), poet and translator, was born in South Bend, Indiana. While living in San Francisco in the late 1940s and 1950s, Rexroth hosted literary salons and philosophical club meetings in his home, as well as a weekly radio show—all of which brought him in contact with poets and writers who eventually would come to be associated with the Beats and the San Francisco Renaissance. Among his many collections of poems are *Collected Shorter Poems* (1967), *Collected Longer Poems* (1968), and *The Complete Poems of Kenneth Rexroth* (2002). Among his translations are *100 Poems from the Chinese* (1956), *100 Poems from the Japanese* (1964), *Pierre Reverdy: Selected Poems* (1969), *100 More Poems from the Chinese: Love and the Turning Year* (1970), and *100 More Poems from the Japanese* (1976). Linda Hamalian has written an excellent biography, *A Life of Kenneth Rexroth* (1992).

RUBY RIEMER taught philosophy at several universities, including Drew University and The New School, during a career that spanned from 1956 to 1990. Her poems, reviews, articles, and essays have been published in many magazines and journals. She lives in Green Village, New Jersey, about thirty miles west of Rutherford.

JUDITH ROBBINS is the minister of the Sheepscott Community Church in the village of Sheepscott, Maine. She writes in her writing house, built between field and woods, on her property in Whitfield, Maine.

CAROLYN FOSTER SEGAL teaches creative writing, American literature, and film at Cedar Crest College in Allentown, Pennsylvania. Her poems, essays, and fiction have appeared in the *Chronicle of Higher Education*, *Inside Higher Ed.*, *2River View*, and *Long Island Quarterly*. Her recent scholarly work has focused on trauma studies, including a paper, "'So Much Depends Upon—': Trauma Narratives in the Poems of William Carlos Williams."

HARVEY SHAPIRO's many books include *The Sights Along the Harbor: New and Collected Poems* (2009), *How Charlie Shavers Died and Other Poems* (2001), and *National Cold Storage Company* (1988). He published his first book in 1953, and has taught at Cornell University, Bard College, Columbia University, and Yale University. In his career as a journalist, he has served as editor of the *New York Times Book Review* and senior editor of the *New York Times Magazine*. He lives in Brooklyn, New York.

MIKE SMITH is a graduate of the University of North Carolina at Greensboro, Hollins College, and the University of Notre Dame. He is the author of *How to Make a Mummy* (2008). His poems have appeared in *Carolina Quarterly*, *Hotel Amerika*, *North American Review*, *Quarter After Eight*, *Notre Dame Review*, *Salt*, *DIAGRAM*, and *Borderlands*.

MARY ELLEN SOLT (1920–2007) was born in Gilmore, Iowa. She taught in the Department of Comparative Literature at Indiana University for more than two decades, where she was director of the Polish Studies Center. In the late 1950s she began corresponding with Williams, and the two became close friends—in fact, Williams traveled to Bloomington in 1960 to hear Solt deliver her lecture, "William Carlos Williams: The American Idiom." Solt is also well known for her work as a concrete poet and as an editor of concrete poetry. Her collection of poems, *Flowers in Concrete*, appeared in 1966, and with Willis Barnstone she edited the pioneering anthology *Concrete Poetry: A World View* (1968). Her extensive collection of visual and concrete poetry is archived in the Lilly Library at Indiana University.

JACK SPICER (1925–1965) was born in Los Angeles and studied linguistics, Anglo-Saxon, and Old Norse at the University of California, Berkeley. In 1950 he lost his teaching assistantship after refusing to sign a "loyalty oath" to the United States, which the University of California required of all its employees under the Sloan-Levering Act. Spicer taught briefly at the University of Minnesota and worked in the rare books room at the Boston Public Library. He lived the majority of his life in San Francisco working as a researcher in linguistics. Active in the poetry and art scenes during the 1950s and 1960s, he is often associated with the writers of the San Francisco Renaissance. *The Collected Books of Jack Spicer* was published in 1975. More recently, Peter Gizzi and Kevin Killian edited *My Vocabulary Did This to Me: The Collected Poetry of Jack Spicer* (2008); Gizzi also edited *The House That Jack Built: The Collected Lectures of Jack Spicer* (1998); and Lewis Ellingham and Kevin Killian wrote Spicer's biography, *Poet Be Like God: Jack Spicer and the San Francisco Renaissance* (1998).

WILLIAM STAFFORD (1914–1993), born in Hutchinson, Kansas, published more than sixty books of poetry and prose, including *Traveling Through the Dark*, winner of the National Book Award in 1963—other finalists that year were Robert Frost's *In the Clearing* and William Carlos Williams's *Pictures from Brueghel*. Stafford taught at Lewis & Clark College in Portland, Oregon, for more than thirty years, where now the William Stafford Archive is located. Among Stafford's many books are *The Way It Is: New and Selected Poems* (1998); *Writing the Australian Crawl*, interviews and essays (1978); and *Down in My Heart*, a memoir (1947). Recent collections of Stafford's poems and essays include *Another World Instead: The Early Poems of William Stafford 1937–1947*, edited by Fred Marchant (2008); *Every War Has Two Losers: William Stafford on Peace and War* (2003); and Kim Stafford's, *Early Morning: Remembering My Father, William Stafford* (2002). *Every War Has Two Losers*, a documentary film based on the journals of William Stafford directed by Haydn Reiss, was released in 2009.

WALLACE STEVENS (1879–1955) was born in Reading, Pennsylvania. He left Harvard after two years because of family finances, and eventually graduated from the New York School of Law in 1903. He was a successful insurance lawyer with several New York companies, and in 1916 he went to work for the Hartford Accident and Indemnity Company, where he remained employed for the rest of his life, becoming vice president in 1934. Among his collections of poems are *Harmonium* (1923; rev. 1931), *Ideas of Order* (1935, enlarged ed., 1936), *Notes Toward a Supreme Fiction* (1942), and *The Palm at the End of the Mind: Selected Poems and a Play by Wallace Stevens*, edited by Holly Stevens (1971). *Wallace Stevens: Collected Poetry and Prose* was published in 1997. Stevens wrote the preface to Williams's *Collected Poems, 1921–1931* (1934). Williams struggled with Stevens's assessment of Williams as a romantic and antipoetic poet and never allowed the preface to be reprinted in his work, though it can be found in Steven's *Opus Posthumous: Poems, Plays, Prose* (1986).

JOHN STONE (1936–2008) was born in Jackson, Mississippi. He is the author of eight collections of poems, including *In All This Rain* (1980), *Renaming the Streets* (1985), *The Smell of Matches* (1988), *Where Water Begins* (1998), and *Music from Apartment 8: New and Selected Poems* (2004), and the essay collection *In the Country of Hearts: Journeys in the Art of Medicine* (1990). He co-edited *On Doctoring* (2001), an anthology of literature and medicine that, since 1991, has been presented to every student entering a U.S. medical school as a gift from the Robert Wood Johnson Foundation. He wrote the libretto for the choral symphony *Canticles of Time* and performed in 2001 at Carnegie Hall in a program titled "The Poet and the Pianist." Until his death in 2008, he was professor of medicine (cardiology) emeritus at Emory University School of Medicine, and for nineteen years director of admissions and associate dean at the school.

YUKO TANIGUCHI was born in Yokohama, Japan. At the age of fifteen, she came to the United States and attended high school in Maryland. She earned her undergraduate degree at the College of St. Benedict/St. John's University and her M.F.A. from the University of Minnesota. Her first volume of poetry, *Foreign Wife Elegy* (2004), was the recipient of an American Book Award, and her first novel, *The Ocean in the Closet*, was published in 2007. She lives in Rochester, Minnesota.

CHARLES TOMLINSON was born in 1927 in Stoke-on-Trent and studied English at Cambridge University. He taught at Bristol University for many years, becoming emeritus professor of English literature. In 1957 Hugh Kenner introduced Williams to Tomlinson when he shared one of Tomlinson's poems—dedicated to Williams and written in triadic lines—that was published in the literary magazine where Kenner was teaching. Among Tomlinson's many poetry collections are *A Peopled Landscape* (1963), *American Scenes, and Other Poems* (1966), *Notes from New York and Other Poems* (1984), *Collected Poems* (1988), *Annunciations* (1998), *The Vineyard Above the Sea* (2000), *Skywriting* (2003), *Selected Poems: 1995–1997* (1997), *Cracks in the Universe* (2006), and *New Collected Poems* (2009). He is the editor of *The Oxford Book of Verse in English Translation* (1980) and has translated the work of many poets, including Italian poet Attilio Bertolucci and Mexican poet Octavio Paz. His prose includes *Poetry and Metamorphosis* (1983) and *Metamorphoses: Poetry and Translation* (2003). *William Carlos Williams and Charles Tomlinson: A Transatlantic Connection*, edited by Barry Magid and Hugh Witemeyer, was published in 1998.

GAEL TURNBULL (1928–2004) was born in Edinburgh, Scotland, and grew up in England and Canada. He read natural science at Cambridge University and studied medicine at the University of Pennsylvania, where he received his M.D. in 1951. He worked as a general practitioner and anesthetist in Canada, the United States, and England. In 1957 he founded Migrant Press, which published the work of the second-generation modernist American and British poets. He is often thought of as a transatlantic bridge to the new poetics of the 1950s and 1960s. "A Visit to WCW: September, 1958," a memoir of Turnbull's visit with Williams at 9 Ridge Road, was published in the winter 1962 issue of the *Massachusetts Review*. Among Turnbull's collections of poems are *A Trampoline: Poems 1952–1964* (1968) and *Scantlings: Poems 1964–69* (1970). *There Are Words: Collected Poems* was published in 2006, and a forthcoming collection of his letters is due in 2011.

JUDITH VALENTE is an on-air correspondent for PBS-TV and Chicago Public Radio and contributing correspondent for National Public Radio. She worked previously as a staff writer for the *Wall Street Journal*, the *Washington Post*, and *People* magazine. She is the author of the poetry chapbook *Inventing an Alphabet*, selected by Mary Oliver for the 2004 Aldrich Poetry Prize, and co-editor with her husband, Charles Reynard, of *Twenty Poems to Nourish Your Soul* (2005), an anthology of poems and reflections on finding the sacred in the every day, winner of a 2008 Eric Hoffer Book Award citation.

KATRINA VANDENBERG's first book, *Atlas* (2004), was a finalist for the Minnesota Book Award. With poet Todd Boss, she is coauthor of a fine-arts chapbook, *On Marriage*. She is the recipient of a Fulbright Fellowship to the Netherlands, a Bush Artist Fellowship in Literature, and a Loft-McKnight Award in Poetry. Most recently, she was the resident fellow at the Amy Clampitt House in Lenox, Massachusetts. She lives in St. Paul, Minnesota, where she teaches in the M.F.A. program at Hamline University.

BYRON VAZAKAS (1905–1987) was born in New York, his father a Greek immigrant and his mother from Reading, Pennsylvania. Self-taught, Vazakas lived most of his life in Reading, becoming friends with the abstract expressionist painter William Baziotes, another Reading resident of Greek ancestry. Vazakas wrote to William Carlos Williams, and the two became pen pals. Williams found a publisher for Vazakas's first collection of poetry, *Transfigured Night* (1946), and wrote the introduction, calling Vazakas, "that important phenomenon among writers, an inventor," and characterized him as "gentle-vitriolic, kind-inhuman, forgiving-obdurate, a poet whose urbanity is inviolate." Williams's letters to Vazakas can be found in the Beinecke Rare Book and Manuscript Library at Yale University, and Vazakas's papers are archived at Albright College in Reading. Two of Vazakas's poems appear in *American Poetry: The Twentieth Century*, Vol. 2, *e. e. cummings to May Swenson* (2000). *Nostalgias for a House of Cards* (1970) was his last collection of poems.

CHUCK WACHTEL is the author of the novels *Joe the Engineer* (1994) and *The Gates* (1996); a collection of stories and novellas, *Because We Were Here* (1996); and five collections of poems and short prose, including *The Coriolis Effect* (1985) and *What Happens to Me* (2000). He teaches in the creative writing program at New York University.

DAVI WALDERS's poetry and prose have appeared in more than 200 anthologies and journals. She developed and directs the Vital Signs Writing Project at the National Institutes of Health in Bethesda, Maryland. Her awards include a National Endowment for the Humanities Grant, a Maryland State Artist Grant in Poetry, a Luce Foundation Grant, and fellowships to Ragdale Foundation, Blue Mountain Center, and Virginia Center for the Creative Arts. She lives in Chevy Chase, Maryland.

ERNEST WALSH (1895–1926) was born in Detroit and spent his childhood in Cuba, where his father was a coffee merchant. Walsh left home at the age of fourteen. At seventeen, he was diagnosed with tuberculosis and spent two years in a sanatorium in New York. Walsh enlisted in the army in 1917 and was severely injured in a training flight of the plane he was piloting in Texas. He began writing poetry during his recovery and published work in *Poetry*. After leaving the hospital, he moved to Paris in the early 1920s, where he, along with Kay Boyle and Ethel Moorhead, edited *This Quarter*, an English-language review of art and literature, and one of the leading little literary magazines of the time, publishing work by James Joyce, Djuna Barnes, H.D., Ernest Hemingway, Gertrude Stein, and William Carlos Williams. While she was separated from her husband, Kay Boyle and Walsh had a daughter together. Walsh's poems were collected in *Poems and Sonnets: With a Memoir by Ethel Moorhead* (1935).

JONATHAN WILLIAMS (1929–2008) was born in Ashville, North Carolina. He spent a year at Princeton but left to study painting, photography, and book design on his own. Eventually he enrolled at Black Mountain College in 1951, studied with Charles Olson, and founded his legendary Jargon Society, publishing more than a hundred books during its long and distinguished history. Over a thousand of his own poems are collected in *Jubilant Thicket: New and Selected Poems* (2005).

ELIZABETH WILLIS's most recent book of poems is *Address* (2011). Other collections include *Meteoric Flowers* (2006), *Turneresque* (2003), and *The Human Abstract* (1995). She edited a collection of essays titled *Radical Vernacular: Lorine Niedecker and the Poetics of Place* (2008). Her essays on twentieth-century literature and culture have appeared in *Textual Practice*, *Contemporary Literature*, *Arizona Quarterly*, and *XCP: Cross-cultural Poetics*. She teaches at Wesleyan University and lives in Holyoke, Massachusetts.

YVOR WINTERS (1900–1968) was born in Chicago. He taught for nearly four decades at Stanford University, where he influenced many young writers, among them J. V. Cunningham, N. Scott Momaday, Thom Gunn, Donald Hall, Robert Hass, Philip Levine, and Robert Pinsky. Recent editions of his work include *Yvor Winters: Selected Poems*, edited by Thom Gunn (2003), and *Selected Poems of Yvor Winters* (1999) and *Selected Letters of Yvor Winters* (2000), both edited by R. L. Barth. While much of Winters's early poetry was influenced by Williams, the Imagists, and the experimental trends of the modernist movement, eventually Winters turned to embrace a more formalist and moralist aesthetic.

DAVID WOJAHN was born in St. Paul, Minnesota. His most recent collection, *Interrogation Palace: New and Selected Poems 1982–2004* (2006), was a finalist for the Pulitzer Prize. He is the author of *Spirit Cabinet* (2002), *The Falling Hour* (1997), *Late Empire* (1994), *Mystery Train* (1990), and *Glassworks* (1987). His first book, *Icehouse Lights* (1982), was selected by Richard Hugo as the winner of the Yale Series of Younger Poets Prize in 1982, and it also was the recipient of the William Carlos Williams Book Award from the Poetry Society of America. He is professor of English and director of creative writing at Virginia Commonwealth University and also teaches in the low-residency M.F.A. in Writing program at Vermont College of Fine Arts.

C. DALE YOUNG practices medicine full time, serves as poetry editor of the *New England Review*, and teaches in the Warren Wilson College M.F.A. Program for Writers. He is the author of *The Day Underneath the Day* (2001), *The Second Person* (2007), and *TORN* (forthcoming in 2011). In 2009 he received a creative writing fellowship from the National Endowment for the Arts. His poems have appeared in many anthologies and magazines, including *The Best American Poetry*, *Asian American Poetry: The Next Generation*, *Legitimate Dangers: American Poets of the New Century*, *American Poetry Review*, *Paris Review*, *Ploughshares*, and *Poetry*.

DAVID P. YOUNG—poet, translator, editor, scholar, and teacher—is the author of ten collections of poems, including, most recently, *Black Lab* (2006) and *The Planet on the Desk: Selected and New Poems 1960–1990* (1991). In 1969 he was a founding editor of *Field: Contemporary Poetry and Poetics*, one of the longest surviving and most important and influential poetry journals of the past fifty years.

GEORGE YOUNG is a retired internist/rheumatologist, having worked at the Boulder Medical Center for thirty-two years. His first collection of poems, *Spinoza's Mouse* (1996), won the Washington Prize. His poems have been included in two anthologies of poems by physicians, *Blood and Bone* (1998) and *Primary Care: More Poems by Physicians* (2006).

VASSILIS ZAMBARAS was born in Greece, and at the age of four moved with his parents to Raymond, Washington, in 1948. He graduated from the University of Washington, where he received an M.A. in English. In 1970 he cofounded the poetry magazine *Madrona* and also worked for the Seattle Housing Authority before returning to Greece in 1972. Since 1977 he has taught English as a second language in his language school in Messenias, Greece. He is the author of two collections of poetry, *Sentences* (1976) and *Aural* (1984).

DAVID ZAUHAR lives in Greensburg, Pennsylvania, and is the author of two chapbooks of poetry, *EconoPoem* and *PoemEcono*. He is at work on a book, currently titled "God and the Beat Generation."

BILL ZAVATSKY's most recent books are a collection of poems, *Where X Marks the Spot* (2006) and a cotranslation (with Ron Padgett) of *The Poems of* A. O. *Barnabooth* by Valery Larbaud (2008). He teaches high school English at the Trinity School in New York.

KIP ZEGERS has taught since 1984 at Hunter College High School in New York City. He is the author of two collections of poems, *The Landmark*, winner of the 2002 Two Rivers Poetry Prize (2003), and *Walt's Last Stand* (2005).

permissions

We are grateful to the authors, editors, publishers, and literary estate executors who have granted us permission to reprint the poems in this anthology.

A. R. AMMONS, "WCW." From *Briefings: Poems Small and Easy*. New York: W. W. Norton & Company, Inc., 1971. Copyright © 1971 by A. R. Ammons. Used by permission of W. W. Norton & Company, Inc.

RANE ARROYO, "The Carlos Poems." From *The Singing Shark*. Tempe, Ariz.: Bilingual Review Press, 1996. Copyright © 1996 by Rane Arroyo. Reprinted by permission of the author.

JOHN ASHBERY, "The Thief of Poetry." From *Houseboat Days*. Copyright © 1975, 1976, 1977, 1999 by John Ashbery. Reprinted by permission of Georges Borchardt, Inc., on behalf of the author.

TONY BARNSTONE, "Appetite." Copyright © 2008 by Tony Barnstone. Reprinted by permission of the author.

WILLIS BARNSTONE, "William Carlos Williams Back in Puerto Rico." From *Algebra of Night: New and Selected Poems 1948–1998*. New York: Sheep Meadow Press, 1999. Copyright © 1999 by Willis Barnstone. Reprinted by permission of the author.

DENNIS BARONE, "Prescriptions." From *Parallel Lines*. Scottsdale, Ariz.: Star Cloud Press, 2011. Copyright © 2011 by Dennis Barone. Reprinted by permission of the author.

JEFFERY BEAM, "What I Know about Poetry." From *Visions of Dame Kind*. Winston-Salem, N.C.: The Jargon Society, 1995. Copyright © 1995 by Jeffery Beam. Reprinted by permission of the author.

MARVIN BELL, "The Book of the Dead Man (The Red Wheelbarrow)" first appeared in *Boulevard* 26, no. 1 (Spring 2010). Copyright © 2010 by Marvin Bell. Published by permission of the author.

CHARLES BERNSTEIN, "For Bill Charley Bill on Memorial Day" first appeared in the *Literary Review* (Fall 2004), Innovative Poetry Feature, guest edited by John Kinsella. Copyright © 2004 by Charles Bernstein. Reprinted by permission of the author.

TED BERRIGAN, "Sonnet XV." From *The Sonnets* by Ted Berrigan. Copyright © 2000 by Alice Notley, Literary Executrix of the Estate of Ted Berrigan. Used by permission of Viking Penguin, a division of Penguin Group (USA) Inc.

ELEANOR BERRY, "Taking the Field." From *Just Before Igniting: Poems*. Salem, Ore.: The Peregrine Writers, 2003. Copyright © 2003 by Eleanor Berry. Reprinted by permission of the author.

WENDELL BERRY, "In a Motel Parking Lot, Thinking of Dr. Williams." From *The Selected Poems of Wendell Berry*. Berkeley, Calif.: Counterpoint, LLC. Copyright © 1999 by Wendell Berry. Reprinted by permission of Counterpoint.

JOHN BERRYMAN, "Dream Song #324: An Elegy for W.C.W., the lovely man." From *The Dream Songs*. New York: Farrar, Straus and Giroux, LLC. Copyright © 1969 by John Berryman. Copyright renewed by Kate Donahue Berryman. Reprinted by permission of the publisher.

PAUL BLACKBURN, "Phone Call to Rutherford." From *Selected Poems of Paul Blackburn*. New York: Persea Books, 1989. Copyright © 1963 by Paul Blackburn. Reprinted by permission of the publisher.

ROBERT BLY, "A Dream of William Carlos Williams." From *Gratitude to Old Teachers*. Brockport, N.Y.: BOA Editions, 1993. Copyright © 1993 by Robert Bly. Reprinted by permission of the author.

KAY BOYLE, "Two Twilights for William Carlos Williams." From *Collected Poems*. Port Townsend, Wash.: Copper Canyon Press, 1991. Copyright © 1991 by Kay Boyle. Reprinted with permission of Copper Canyon Press, www.coppercanyonpress.org.

RICHARD BRAUTIGAN, "September 3 (The Dr. William Carlos Williams Mistake)." From *Loading Mercury with a Pitchfork*. New York: Simon & Schuster, 1976. Copyright © by Richard Brautigan. Used with permission of the author's estate.

MICHAEL J. BUGEJA, "The Influence of William Carlos Williams." Copyright © 2009 by Michael Bugeja. Reprinted by permission of the author.

JOHN CIARDI, "Bicentennial." From *For Instance*. New York: W. W. Norton & Company, Inc. Copyright © 1979 by John Ciardi. Used by permission of W. W. Norton & Company.

CID CORMAN, "'WCW & Mary O.'" From *The Next One Thousand Years*. Edited by Bob Arnold and Ce Rosenow. Guilford, Vt.: Longhouse Books, 2008. Copyright © 2008. Reprinted by permission of the publisher.

ROBERT CREELEY, "For W.C.W." From *Selected Poems: 1945–2005*. Berkeley: University of California Press, 2008. Copyright © 2008 by Robert Creeley. Reprinted by permission of the publisher.

BARBARA CROOKER, "Alicia Silverstone Meets William Carlos Williams" first appeared in *Neo/Victorian Cochlea*. Copyright © 2002 by Barbara Crooker. Reprinted by permission of the author.

TODD DAVIS, "Confession." From *The Least of These*. East Lansing: Michigan State University Press, 2000. Copyright © 2009 by Todd Davis. Reprinted by permission of the author.

GREG DELANTY, "Williams Was Wrong." From *Collected Poems: 1986–2006*. Manchester, U.K.: Carcanet Press Limited. Copyright © 2006 by Greg Delanty. Reprinted by permission of the publisher and the author.

THOMAS DISCH, "In Defense of Forest Lawn." From *Yes, Let's: New and Selected Poems*. Baltimore: Johns Hopkins University Press, 1989. Copyright © 1989 by Thomas M. Disch. All rights reserved by the Estate of Thomas M. Disch.

NORMAN DUBIE, "A Physical Moon beyond Paterson." From *The Mercy Seat: Collected and New Poems: 1967–2001*. Port Townsend, Wash.: Copper Canyon Press, 2001. Copyright © by Norman Dubie. Reprinted by permission of the author.

STEPHEN DUNN, "Memory." From *Riffs & Reciprocities: Prose Pairs*. New York: W. W. Norton & Company, Inc. Copyright © 1998 by Stephen Dunn. Used by permission of W. W. Norton & Company, Inc.

RICHARD EBERHART, "To William Carlos Williams." From *Collected Poems: 1930–1986*. New York: Oxford University Press, 1988. Copyright © 1988 by Richard Eberhart. Reprinted by permission of Oxford University Press.

HEID E. ERDRICH, "Some Elsie." From *National Monuments*. East Lansing: Michigan State University Press, 2009. Copyright © 2009 by Heid E. Erdrich. Reprinted by permission of the publisher.

SUSAN FIRER, "Call Me Pier." From *Milwaukee Does Strange Things to People: New & Selected Poems 1979–2007*. Omaha, Neb.: Backwaters Press, 2007. Copyright © 2007 by Susan Firer. Reprinted by permission of the author.

ANN FISHER-WIRTH, "Slow Rain, October." Copyright © 2010 by Ann Fisher-Wirth. Reprinted by permission of the author.

ALICE FRIMAN, "*Ars Poetica* on Lava" first appeared in the *Georgia Review* 48, no. 4 (Winter 2009). Copyright © 2009 by Alice Friman. Reprinted by permission of the author.

ROBERT GIBB, "Williams in Autumn." From *What the Heart Can Bear: Selected and Uncollected Poems, 1977–1993*. Pittsburgh: Autumn House Press, 2009. Copyright © 2009 by Robert Gibb. Reprinted by permission of the author.

ALLEN GINSBERG, "Death News." From *Collected Poems: 1947–1997*. New York: HarperCollins, 2006. Copyright © 1963 by Allen Ginsberg. Reprinted by permission of HarperCollins Publishers.

PETER GIZZI, "The Outernationale." From *The Outernationale*. Middletown, Conn.: Wesleyan University Press, 2007. Copyright © 2007 by Peter Gizzi. Reprinted by permission of the author and the publisher.

SUSAN GLICKMAN, "Saxifrage: To the Memory of William Carlos Williams" first appeared in *Arrivals: Canadian Poetry in the Eighties*, edited by Bruce Meyer. Greenfield Center, N.Y.: Greenfield Review Press, 1986. Copyright © 1986 by Susan Glickman. Reprinted by permission of the author.

DAVID GRAHAM, "Red Wheel Boogie and Dog Star Night." Copyright © 2009 by David Graham. Reprinted by permission of the author.

MICHAEL HEFFERNAN, "An Exculpation." Copyright © 2009 by Michael Heffernan. Reprinted by permission of the author.

WILLIAM HEYEN, "The Confessions of Doc Williams." From *The Confessions of Doc Williams*. Wilkes-Barre, Pa.: Etruscan Press, 2006. Copyright © 2006 by William Heyen. Reprinted by permission of the publisher.

EDWARD HIRSCH, "Liberty Brass" first appeared in the *New Yorker*. Copyright © 2009 by Edward Hirsch. Reprinted by permission of the author.

DANIEL HOFFMAN, "Words for Dr. Williams." From *Beyond Silence: Selected Shorter Poems, 1948–2003*. Copyright © 1968 by Daniel Hoffman. Reprinted by permission of LSU Press.

DAVID IGNATOW, "For WCW." From *At My Ease: Uncollected Poems of the Fifties and Sixties*. Brockport, N.Y.: BOA Editions, 1997. Copyright © 1997 by Yaedi Ignatow. Reprinted by permission of Yaedi Ignatow.

RODNEY JONES, "Plea for Forgiveness." From *Elegy for the Southern Drawl: Poems by Rodney Jones*. Copyright © 1999 by Rodney Jones. Reprinted by permission of Houghton Mifflin Harcourt Publishing Company. All rights reserved.

JACK KEROUAC, "83rd Chorus." From *Mexico City Blues*. New York: Grove Weidenfeld, 1959. Copyright © 1959 by Jack Kerouac. Reprinted by permission of SLL/Sterling Lord Literistic, Inc.

GALWAY KINNELL, "For William Carlos Williams." From *What a Kingdom It Was*. New York: Houghton Mifflin, 1960. Copyright © 1960, renewed 1988 by Galway Kinnell. Reprinted by permission of Houghton Mifflin Harcourt Publishing Company. All rights reserved.

KENNETH KOCH, "Variations on a Theme by William Carlos Williams." From *Collected Poems of Kenneth Koch*. New York: Alfred A. Knopf, 2005. Copyright © 2005 by the Kenneth Koch Literary Estate. Used by permission of Alfred A. Knopf, a division of Random House, Inc.

KAREN KOVACIK, "WCW on Marsden Hartley" first appeared in *Salmagundi*. Copyright © 1999 by Karen Kovacik. Reprinted by permission of the author.

MAXINE KUMIN, "WCW." Copyright © 2009 by Maxine Kumin. Reprinted by permission of the author.

JAMES LAUGHLIN, "So Much Depends." From *The Collected Poems of James Laughlin*. Copyright © 1986 by James Laughlin. Reprinted by permission of New Directions Publishing Corp.

DAVID LEHMAN, "Poem in the Manner of William Carlos Williams" first appeared in *Boulevard* 23, no. 1 (Fall 2007). Copyright © 2007 by David Lehman. Reprinted by permission of the author.

GARY LEISING, "William Carlos Williams at Paterson Falls." Copyright © 2009 by Gary Leising. Reprinted by permission of the author.

DENISE LEVERTOV, "Williams: An Essay." From *Candles in Babylon*. Copyright © 1982 by Denise Levertov. Reprinted by permission of New Direction Publishing Corp.

PHILIP LEVINE, "Making It Work." From *A Walk with Tom Jefferson*. New York: Alfred A. Knopf, 1988. Copyright © 1988 by Philip Levine. Used by permission of Alfred A. Knopf, a division of Random House, Inc.

LYN LIFSHIN, "When People First Said I Must Have Been Influenced by William Carlos Williams." Copyright © 2009 by Lyn Lifshin. Reprinted by permission of the author.

ROBERT LOWELL, "William Carlos Williams." From *Collected Poems*. New York: Farrar, Straus and Giroux, LLC, 2003. Copyright © 2003 by Harriet Lowell and Sheridan Lowell. Reprinted by permission of the publisher.

LEZA LOWITZ, "*Eka Pada Rajakapotasana*: One Legged King Pigeon Pose." From *Yoga Poems: Lines to Unfold By*. Berkeley, Calif.: Stone Bridge Press, 2006. Copyright © 2006 by Leza Lowitz. Reprinted by permission of the author.

CLARENCE MAJOR, "The Young Doctor (1916)." From *Myself Painting*. Copyright © 2008 by Clarence Major. Reprinted by permission of LSU Press.

PAUL MARIANI, "Elegy for William Carlos Williams on the Eve of His 125th Birthday" first appeared in *Image*. Copyright © 2009 by Paul Mariani. Reprinted by permission of the author.

JOSEPH MASSEY, "From a Window." From *Eureka Slough*. Austin, Tex.: Effing Press, 2005. Copyright © 2005 by Joseph Massey. Reprinted by permission of the author.

PANSY MAURER-ALVAREZ, "On Reading 'Days and Nights' by Kenneth Koch" first appeared in *Hanging Loose*, no. 66 (1995). Copyright © 1995 by Pansy Maurer-Alvarez. Reprinted by permission of the author.

JAMES MERRILL, "From the Cutting-Room Floor." From *Collected Poems*. Edited by J. D. McClatchy and Stephen Yenser. Copyright © 2001 by the Literary Estate of James Merrill at Washington University. Used by permission of Alfred A. Knopf, a division of Random House, Inc.

JOE MILUTIS, "By Defective Means." Copyright © 2009 by Joe Milutis. Reprinted by permission of the author.

HILDA MORLEY, "For W. C. Williams." From *Cloudless at First*. Mt. Kisko, N.Y.: Moyer Bell Limited, 1988. Copyright © 1988 by Hilda Morley. Reprinted by permission of the publisher.

JOYCE CAROL OATES, "This Is the Time for Which We Have Been Waiting" first appeared in *The Humanist* 68, no. 4 (July/August 2008). Copyright © 2008 by *The Ontario Review*, Inc. Reprinted by permission of the author.

FRANK O'HARA, "To a Poet." From *The Collected Poems of Frank O'Hara*. Edited by Donald Allen. Copyright © 1971 by Maureen Granville-Smith, Administratrix of the Estate of Frank O'Hara. Copyright renewed 1999 by Maureen Granville-Smith and Donald Allen. Used by permission of Alfred A. Knopf, a division of Random House, Inc.

CHARLES OLSON, "Red Mallows." From *The Collected Poems of Charles Olson*. Edited by George F. Butterick. Berkeley: University of California Press, 1997. Copyright © 1987 by the Estate of Charles Olson. Reprinted by permission of the Estate of Charles Olson.

JOEL OPPENHEIMER, "We Mark the Centennial of William Carlos Williams' Birth Observing a New Hampshire Patriot." From *Collected Later Poems of Joel Oppenheimer*. Edited by Robert J. Bertholf. Buffalo: SUNY-Buffalo, The Poetry/Rare Books Collection 1997. Copyright © 1997 by The Literary Estate of Joel Oppenheimer.

LOUIS PHILLIPS, "A Critical Glance at William Carlos Williams' Poem, 'The Dance.'" Copyright © 2009 by Louis Phillips. Reprinted by permission of Louis Phillips.

EZRA POUND, excerpt from "Canto LXXVIII" (from *The Pisan Cantos*). Copyright © 1948 by Ezra Pound. Reprinted by permission of New Direction Press.

TONY QUAGLIANO, "For Doctor WCW" first appeared in *JAMA: The Journal of the American Medical Association* 268, no. 21 (December 2, 1992). Copyright © 1992 by Tony Quagliano. Reprinted by permission of Laura Ruby, Literary Executor for Tony Quagliano.

F. D. REEVE, "Violets in a Pewter Vase." From *The Puzzle Master and Other Poems*. New York: New York Quarterly Books, 2010. Copyright © 2010 by F. D. Reeve. Reprinted by permission of the author.

KENNETH REXROTH, "A Letter to William Carlos Williams." From *The Collected Shorter Poems*. Copyright © 1950 by Kenneth Rexroth. Reprinted by permission of New Directions Publishing Corp.

RUBY RIEMER, "W.C.W.—In Memoriam" first appeared in *Exquisite Corpse*, June 10, 1988. Copyright © 1988 by Ruby Riemer. Reprinted by permission of the author.

JUDITH ROBBINS, "Fragment" first appeared in the *American Scholar* 70, no. 1 (Winter 2001). Copyright © 2001 by Judith Robbins. Reprinted by permission of the author.

CAROLYN FOSTER SEGAL, "Mullens." Copyright © 2009 by Carolyn Foster Segal. Reprinted by permission of the author.

HARVEY SHAPIRO, "For WCW." From *National Cold Storage Company: New and Selected Poems*. Middleton, Conn.: Wesleyan University Press, 1988. Copyright © 2001 by Harvey Shapiro. Reprinted by permission of Wesleyan University Press.

MIKE SMITH, "From the Desk of William Carlos Williams: Notes Toward a Speech in Three Parts" first appeared *DIAGRAM* 5, no. 4, and was later collected in the electronic chapbook *Anagrams of America*, published by *Mudlark: Electronic Journal of Poetry and Poetics*, no. 30 (2006). Copyright © 2006 by Mike Smith. Reprinted by permission of the author.

MARY ELLEN SOLT, "For William Carlos Williams" first appeared in *Beloit Poetry Journal* 14, no. 1 (1963). Copyright © 1960 by Mary Ellen Solt. Reprinted by permission of Susan Solt, Literary Executor of the Estate of Mary Ellen Solt.

JACK SPICER, "A Red Wheelbarrow." From *My Vocabulary Did This to Me: The Collected Poetry of Jack Spicer*. Edited by Peter Gizzi and Kevin Killian. Middletown, Conn.: Wesleyan University Press, 2008. Copyright © 2008 by the Estate of Jack Spicer. Reprinted by permission of the publisher.

WILLIAM STAFFORD, "*Understanding Poetry*, by William Carlos Williams and Wallace Stevens" first appeared in *South Coast Poetry Journal*, no. 4 (Fall 1987). Copyright © 1987 by William Stafford. Reprinted by permission of the Estate of William Stafford.

WALLACE STEVENS, "Nuances of a Theme by Williams." From *The Collected Poems of Wallace Stevens*. Copyright © 1954 by Wallace Stevens and renewed 1982 by Holly Stevens. Used by permission of Alfred A. Knopf, a division of Random House, Inc.

JOHN STONE, "Getting to Sleep in New Jersey." From *Music from Apartment 8: New and*

Selected Poems. Baton Rouge: LSU Press, 2004. Copyright © 2004 by John Stone. Reprinted by permission of the publisher.

YUKO TANIGUCHI, "Turning." From *Foreign Wife Elegy*. Minneapolis, Minn.: Coffee House Press, 2004. Copyright © 2004 by Yuko Taniguchi. Reprinted by permission of the author.

CHARLES TOMLINSON, "Remembering Williams." From *New Collected Poems*. Manchester, England: Carcanet Press, Ltd., 1985. Copyright © 1984, 1985 by Charles Tomlinson. Reprinted by permission of the publisher.

GAEL TURNBULL, "A Confession" first appeared in *Beloit Poetry Journal* 14, no. 1 (1963). Copyright © 1963 by Gael Turnbull. Reprinted by permission of Jill Turnbull, Literary Executor of the Estate of Gael Turnbull.

JUDITH VALENTE, "Walking with Dr. Williams." From *Discovering Moons*. Chicago: Visual Artists Collective, 2009. Copyright © 2009 by Judith Valente. Reprinted by permission of the author.

KATRINA VANDENBERG, "Plums." Copyright © 2009 by Katrina Vandenberg. Reprinted by permission of the author.

BYRON VAZAKAS, "The Nostalgias of Change." From *Nostalgias for a House of Cards*. New York: October House, 1970. Copyright © 1963 by Byron Vazakas. Reprinted by permission of the Special Collections Archives, Albright College.

CHUCK WACHTEL, "Old Sycamore." From *What Happens to Me: Poems and Short Prose*. New York: Hanging Loose Press, 2001. Copyright © 2001 by Chuck Wachtel. Reprinted by permission of the author.

DAVI WALDERS, "Not in ideas . . ." Copyright © 2009 by Davi Walders. Reprinted with permission of the author.

ERNEST WALSH, "Doctor Bill Williams." From *Poems and Sonnets by Ernest Walsh: With a Memoir by Ethel Moorhead*. New York: Harcourt, Brace & Company, Inc., 1934. Copyright © 1934 and renewed 1962 by Harcourt, Inc. Reprinted by permission of Houghton Mifflin Harcourt Publishing Company.

JONATHAN WILLIAMS, "For William Carlos Williams" first appeared in *Beloit Poetry Journal* 14, no. 1 (1963). Copyright © 1963 by Jonathan Williams. Reprinted by permission of the Estate of Jonathan Williams.

ELIZABETH WILLIS, "The Oldest Garden in the World" first appeared in *Boston Review* 32, no. 6 (November/December 2007). Copyright © 2007 by Elizabeth Willis. Reprinted by permission of the author.

YVOR WINTERS, "Song." From *The Bare Hills*. Boston: Four Seas Co., 1927. Copyright © 1927 by Yvor Winters. Reprinted by permission of Ohio University Press/Swallow Press.

DAVID WOJAHN, "W.C.W. Watching Presley's Second Appearance on *The Ed Sullivan Show*: Mercy Hospital, Newark, 1956." From *Mystery Train*. Copyright © 1990 by David Wojahn. Reprinted by permission of the University of Pittsburgh Press.

C. DALE YOUNG, "Homage to William Carlos Williams." From *The Day Underneath the Day*. Evanston, Ill.: TriQuarterly Books/Northwestern University Press, 2006. Copyright © 2006 by C. Dale Young. Reprinted by permission of the publisher.

DAVID P. YOUNG, "Homage to William Carlos Williams." From *At the White Window*. Columbus: Ohio State University Press, 2000. Copyright © 2000 by David P. Young. Reprinted by permission of the author.

GEORGE YOUNG, "A Letter to William Carlos Williams." From *Spinoza's Mouse*. Washington, D.C.: Word Works, Inc., 1996. Copyright © 1992 by George Young. Reprinted by permission of the author.

VASSILIS ZAMBARAS, "Bookmark, *Selected Poems*, William Carlos Williams." Copyright © 2010 by Vassilis Zambaras. Reprinted by permission of the author.

DAVID ZAUHAR, "Commercial Poem" first appeared in *Exquisite Corpse* 5, no. 9 (1987). Copyright © 1987 by David Zauhar. Reprinted by permission of the author.

BILL ZAVATSKY, "Keats to Williams." Copyright © 2009 by Bill Zavatsky. Printed by permission of the author.

KIP ZEGERS, "Facing It" first appeared in *Beloit Poetry Journal* 49, no. 4 (Summer 1999). Copyright © 1999 by Kip Zegers. Reprinted by permission of the author.

index to titles